G000020093

How was it for you?

Eyewitness accounts from Warwickshire men
and women in the service of their country

FRED STEELE.

John Stanfield faced a crowd of 100,000 which came to the Forbidden City to see the surrender signed.

How was it for you?

Eyewitness accounts from Warwickshire men
and women in the service of their country

Compiled by

Aubrey Chalmers

BREWIN BOOKS

First published by Brewin Books Ltd
Studley, Warwickshire B80 7LG in 2002
www.brewinbooks.com

© *The Royal British Legion Warwickshire,
Contributors and Aubrey Chalmers 2002*

All rights reserved

ISBN 1-85858-210-5 Paperback

The moral right of the authors has been asserted

British Library Cataloguing in Publication Data
A Catalogue record for this book is available from the British Library

All royalties arising from the sale of this book are
being donated to The Royal British Legion Warwickshire

Printed by SupaPrint (Redditch) Limited,
Unit 19, Enfield Industrial Estate, Redditch, Worcs, B97 6BZ.
www.supaprint.com

Contents

The Britons readily submit to military service,
payment of tribute and other obligations imposed
by government, provided that there is no abuse . . .
they are broken in to obedience but not as yet to slavery.

TACITUS AD 55-115

Front Cover image: Roy Scott *(3rd left back row)* with his crew and their Stirling
bomber. They flew missions for SOE dropping spies and supplies to the resistance
fighters and agents.

Acknowledgements

I must express my appreciation to all the contributors and especially to those who have already set down their experiences. Unfortunately a few people have died and will not see the result of their work. In some cases it has been necessary to use extracts from somewhat longer narratives which, in themselves, represent a complete book.

Some contributors have kindly given permission for the use of copyright material.

Fred Frost has given me permission to use extracts from his book *There and Back* and Henry O'Kane has permitted me to use portions from *O'Kane's Korea*. Mrs Iris Herwin has kindly provided a transcript of the immensely valuable secret diary her late husband kept during his two and a half years as a POW. His comments, on rereading his diary in 1992, have amplified some of the rather sparse notes he made some half a century earlier.

The Rev John Stanfield has been kind enough to provide me with a copy of the narrative he wrote following his years in China with the SOE, *China. Special Operations Executive 1943-45,* and Martyn Richards has permitted me to quote from his moving story *Last Letter Home,* the tragic note written by a WW1 soldier before he was executed.

Branch Secretaries have been particularly helpful in making initial contact with potential contributors and others, including Bob Curry from Knowle, have been enthusiastic supporters in assisting with the collection of reminiscences.

Apart from the narratives from members of the Royal British Legion in Warwickshire, I felt it appropriate to include one or two gripping stories from former members of the county regiment, the Royal Warwickshire Regiment. This seemed to be particularly appropriate after meeting two of the survivors of the 1940 Wormhout massacre when they revisited the site on the 60th anniversary and talked me through their horrific ordeal. Alastair Bannerman, has permitted me to use an extract from his lovely book of poetry and prose *As With Your Shadow* in which he describes his capture following the Normandy landings.

I am also grateful for assistance from local historian John Ashby and also the Imperial War Museum which has helped to solve problems over POWs, and also permitted me to reproduce the picture of Pte. Joe Curry which was identified by his family from a somewhat grainy WW1 film. St. John's House Warwick, the Area Headquarters of the Royal Regiment of Fusiliers into which the Royal Warwickshire Regiment was merged, have been most helpful. Finally, I appreciate the encouragement, help and support from the publisher Alan Brewin.

Notes on the Text

Although it has been possible to check most events and locations, the memories of veterans tend to be less reliable as they advance in years. It has proved impossible to verify some place names mentioned in this book, particularly in Silesia and Poland. Some villages, and even towns, are too small to appear on maps and the names of other places have been changed over the years. In some instances troops developed their own form of shorthand to identify far away places which they found difficult to pronounce and even more difficult to spell. Therefore, in many cases, the spelling of locations remains as it was in the original text. I have added, in italics, notes which help to explain or place items in their historical context.

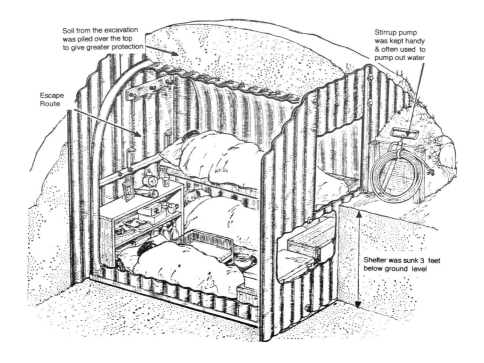

The Anderson Shelter which protected the lives of many civilian families during the heavy bombing of World War II.

Introduction - Service, not Self

Almost anyone who has served in the Armed Forces and similar uniformed organisations has a story to tell.

Frequently military service is the highlight in a person's life. It is a period when, within a disciplined context, they forge new friendships, experience an alien environment, share unusual experiences, seek adventure, enjoy fun, tolerate boredom, face danger, giggle at officialdom and, for some, succeed in surviving extreme privation.

Unwittingly, every former serviceman or woman carries a little piece of history in his or her pocket. The fragment is just a small part of an immensely colourful landscape, a montage composed from each individual's experiences of a unique lifestyle.

It was while I was producing a regimental magazine that I realised that many of the contributions from old soldiers made riveting reading. The idea developed that among the thousands of members of the Royal British Legion in Warwickshire there must be a treasure trove of stories and anecdotes waiting to be discovered.

I was not disappointed. A number of these stories, which would otherwise disappear in the course of time, have now been preserved for posterity.

Generals and war leaders may write dusty memoirs, provide an overview and, with calculated detachment, describe strategy in volumes which have considerable significance for the historian. The real stories, however, come from those at the sharp end who can produce personal snapshots of everyday life. They reflect the experiences of millions of ordinary people who were plunged into a hostile environment which came to dominate their everyday lives.

Their narratives are powerful and graphic and, with the exception of a POW who kept a secret diary during his two and a half years in captivity, they are told here in retrospect. Therefore they can be seen as being objective.

Life in the Armed Forces is different; it is like no other job. Service men and women are trained to put their lives at risk instantly for the benefit of others. They are ordinary people caught up in extraordinary circumstances and whose identities have been sublimated into a military regime. But a civilian in uniform does not leave the citizen behind. Values of compassion, tolerance, humour and loyalty - even fear - cannot be discarded. These qualities are embodied in some shining bonds of friendship and team spirit. Troops, acutely aware of their responsibilities, struggle to support one another under attack and even in captivity.

That same spirit, the desire to help the less fortunate, gave birth to the Royal British Legion.

Added together, these personal cameos represent an important chunk of our national character and our heritage. They also provide an insight into the day to day lives of people who served their country whether in warfare, on peacetime exercise, or in fulfilling a civilian role during a time of crisis and stress.

They cover a wide period and many different aspects of Service life.

There are family accounts from the First World War; many personal experiences from the Second World War and from other conflicts which blemished the latter part of the last century - from Korea, from Malaysia, and even from the Gulf War.

They do not merely record what it is like to be under attack, in a crippled bomber holed by anti-aircraft fire; in a warship closed up for action under a massive air bombardment, or in close quarter combat in the sweaty jungle. One also has an insight into the long term effects of combat. What it is like to be captured, what it is like to be at the mercy of a cruel and unpredictable enemy, how life itself is cheapened by the corrosive effects of combat and, in extreme circumstances, how civilisation suffers regression and reverts to a sub-human culture in a struggle to survive against impossible odds.

In a society which has become quite averse to risk and in which nobody goes hungry, there is still an oddly enduring fascination with the Second World War. As new source material emerges, however, the interest has switched to the human dimension and a lifestyle which now appears unbelievable.

Younger generations have, thankfully, no experience of total war and the majority of the population now have had little contact with military service. Therefore they are bound to ask parents, grandparents, and older friends and relatives: "How was it for you?"

The closest most people come to any experience of warfare is a form of gung-ho, but sanitised, film on television while they are comfortably seated in a warm home, untouched even by the new thirst for virtual reality. Therefore, some of the narrow escapes from death, strange encounters and hardships, especially those suffered by the survivors of a massacre or by men on death marches as the Nazis evacuated prison camps in the face of the Russian advance, must appear utterly incredible.

A reader can be forgiven for wondering how such a survivor, teetering at the very edge of mortality, could remain totally sane thereafter, far less carry on a normal life and be able to hold down a job.

Inevitably former Prisoners of War have the most graphic memories of their treatment at the hands of the enemy.

The vast difference in the treatment of POWs is surprising. These tales strike a comparison between calculated cruelty in some camps and the gentlemanly treatment of wounded prisoners in others. One wounded man was taken prisoner at Tobruk but ended up as a slave labourer. Another, captured near Dunkirk, was well treated while, just a few miles away, men from the same regiment were massacred by the SS. The stories of two survivors expose the full horror of that atrocity.

One can also compare the crude brutality of guards in a camp in desolate Silesia with the systematic mental cruelty and brainwashing inflicted on prisoners by Chinese Communists in Korea.

Little more than half a century ago wretched columns of starving and ragged figures, shown no mercy by their guards, more or less shuffled an amazing 800 or 900 miles westwards across a devastated Europe in the depth of winter. And some, just a few with sufficient willpower, survived to tell the tale.

The unfathomable depth of their despair and the appalling degradation of human beings makes uncomfortable and terrible reading. But the accounts written by these men represent a monument to their endurance and will to survive. It is pitiable to realise that although they may have been encouraged by the sight of Allied air attacks on the enemy, and despite many prisoners being killed in the raids, at the very moment of liberty they were too weak and bewildered to comprehend their freedom.

At the end of the Second World War most of those demobbed wanted to forget about it and get on with their lives. They were still incredibly young. They went off to fight as fresh-faced youths and returned as men - men with the wisdom of years gained in a few short months and weathered by the sun of foreign lands.

But, as these veterans became older and retired, they have been able to weigh up their experiences and many have come to regard them as fulfilling times, particularly when they are viewed against the moral fabric of current society.

Many former service people wish to forget unpleasant experiences; others find it therapeutic to write down traumatic memories. Most like to recall amusing highlights, rather like people looking through an old photograph album and recollecting old friends and experiences. They discovered they could look back and, in the cinema of the mind, replay those vivid cameos, often involving a close brush with death, and find them entertaining; in retrospect they could say, "We can laugh at it now."

Even a starving POW, traumatised by the theft of his meagre hoard of chocolate, was, years later, surprised by his emotive response. A policeman facing the horrors of the blitz in Birmingham still found amusing anecdotes to offset the experience. Sometimes military personnel, involved in what appeared to be the most mundane tasks, produced the most unexpected results.

The stories we have compiled may be mere fragments of history but contributors have served their country in many different ways, invariably without regard to personal safety or sacrifice.

Each story could be said to reflect the Royal British Legion's motto: "Service not Self".

Aubrey Chalmers

Chapter 1

Join the Forces... and see the World

(as well as getting into many odd situations)

British military personnel, serving around the world, have brought home many souvenirs over the years. Few mementoes are more enduring than memories of unusual events, unusual places and warm-hearted people with whom they struck up friendships.

> *Ah. What a delight to be a soldier!*
> EUGÉNE SCRIBE

Surrender in Peking

> *The war between Japan and China commenced in 1937, two years before that in Europe. It is claimed that 300,000 Chinese were killed in the 1937 Nanjing Massacre.*
>
> *The Japanese surrender in Peking on October 10, 1945, was probably the final major surrender of the war, but, because communications were bad, it was scarcely reported outside China. A month earlier, on September 2, Japan had capitulated on board the* USS Missouri.
>
> *The Rev. John Stanfield was, at that time a Major in the Royal Signals with Special Operations Executive, Force 136, in China. Since he was the senior British officer in Peking he was an official witness to the surrender of the Japanese armies of 47 Divisions in the Forbidden City of the Ming and Ching Emperors.*

The ceremony took place on the Dragon Pavement in front of the Grand Coronation Palace or Hall of Supreme Harmony, the spot where, for the last 500 years, the Emperors of China have come for the announcement of victories. The setting and the day combined to make it as colourful and awe-inspiring as any in China's history.

The Grand Coronation Palace contains the Imperial Dragon Throne and is set at the heart of the Forbidden City. The pillars and walls are of deep crimson; the eaves and woodwork painted and decorated with golden dragons of the Imperial crest. The white marble balustrades and terraces were set off by the flags of the Allies in brilliant sunshine which gleamed on the Imperial yellow glazed tiles on the roofs.

The small British party approached the Forbidden City in a car from the legation quarter, through cheering crowds, and under the triumphal arches hung with the flags of the "Big Four", China, Great Britain, the United States and Russia.

We drove past an endless stream of school children and excited crowds with perspiring soldiers trying to clear a passage for the car, up to the main fortress gate of the Forbidden City, through the centre fifty yard tunnel (opened only for the Emperor before 1911) and out into the Forbidden City.

There, we left the car and crossed the large courtyard, up two flights of steps to the Gate of Supreme Harmony. As we passed through the Gate we saw below us the enormous courtyard in front of the Grand Coronation Palace. This was packed with crowds flowing up to the three flights of marble steps and terraces leading up to the Dragon Pavement with the Grand Coronation Palace beyond.

The terraces were brilliant with flags and, behind the red pillars of the huge Hall, could be seen the flags of China, Great Britain, the United States and Russia, draping the walls on each side of the doorway. The curling roofs were set off by the gilding and painting below.

The sight was breathtaking.

As we made our way down through the line of soldiers and up the three flights to the Dragon pavement, a roar of cheering rose and we felt, for the moment, the focus of the Universe.

There, standing on an Imperial Dragon carpet, was a table with the surrender documents.

The Chinese authorities had wisely allowed plenty of time to assemble, and the groups of representatives, all of them wearing the official red silk tabs, strolled about in the sun and took photographs.

Stately long-gowned Chinese officials, modern Chinese Generals, American

John Stanfield was the official British witness to the final surrender of the war. The Japanese surrendered 47 Divisions in China on October 10, 1945.

Marine and Air Force officers, the British party of an embassy official, a Major and two Captains and a Corporal, mixed with civilian spectators of all nations.

A Chinese General escorted me to sign for the British Army. The documents were four concertina-like books, bound in yellow silk, and apparently made of blotting paper to take the Chinese brush writing.

All this time fresh parties arrived, each heralded by a wave of cheering. A Chinese General started to marshal the official spectators, the foreigners on the left and the Chinese on the right, with backs to the Coronation Palace.

A Chinese guard lined the other sides around the table, space being left in front of the steps and Palace for the Japanese.

When all was ready, the General asked spectators to salute or remove their hats as the War Zone Commander, General Sun Lien Chung, came out of the shadow of the doorway of the Palace into the brilliant sun, followed by his aides.

An aide called for the Japanese delegates to be brought forward.

A roar indicated the progress of the Japanese military party as they walked down the two-hundred yard corridor of the courtyard between 100,000 Chinese.

As they started to climb the three flights of steps, the roar became a triumphal shout. Seven years of subjugation ended by the humbling of those officers about to surrender their swords on the spot where defeated enemies of China have surrendered their symbols of war for the last five-hundred years.

Forming a line in front of General Sun the Japanese came to attention, saluted, and filed to the left where they stood to attention.

The General Commanding the Japanese Armies in China was called to sign the surrender. He walked to the table and signed with the brush pen provided.
General Sun then signed the documents.

The next order was: "You will surrender your swords." With the General leading, the Japanese filed one by one to the table, unhooked their swords, and laid them on the table.

Forming up once more they saluted, turned, and marched off to the right. General Sun saluted and, turning, walked back into the Grand Coronation Palace.
In its dim pillared depth stood the huge Dragon Throne. The spectators were invited to drink toasts to the Allies.

The way out was still a triumphal procession. The crowds still clapped and cheered as we made our way through the vast courts and palaces - out from the 15th and into the 20th century.

One felt drained of emotion, the scene had been too picturesque and colourful for reality; the acres of golden tiles, deep crimson walls, marble balustrades, waving crowds. Such a scene can happen only once and this surrender in China's five-hundred year old Forbidden City must have been, for China, the supreme moment of Japanese defeat.

The Rev John Stanfield

Norwegian "Rock Cakes"

Immediately peace in Europe was declared *HMS Vanity* was ordered to take essential food supplies to British forces in Norway.

On arrival at Stavanger we had to proceed slowly and wait for a German "E" Boat to come out and pilot us into the harbour. A German officer in charge of the craft made her turn on a tanner, very impressive.

Ashore, there were Russian POWs who had been released by the Germans. They were very pleased to see us, as were the Norwegian people. The Russian POWs had not been treated very well by the Germans and, after six years of occupation, the citizens of Norway were living practically at starvation level.

We unloaded some of our "iron rations"and met some army personnel. Within 48 hours we were on our way down to Kristiansand and then to Oslo. We sailed through beautiful fiords with wooden houses dotted among the pine forests. Each small house was proudly flying a Norwegian flag from its own flagpole. Our ship's speakers were turned on fully, playing "Land of Hope and Glory" and "There'll Always be an England."

While in Kristiansand we took over an empty wooden German hall. We practically emptied Jack Dusty's store in order to put on a large buffet and entertain the Norwegian teenagers. The cooks (Singe'em and Burn'em) baked as much bread as they could. We had a great afternoon and, after six years of occupation, our hospitality was really appreciated. Most of the Norwegians spoke good English and I met one girl whose father was a ship owner. I often wondered what became of her and her family.

Our next port of call was Oslo. The sea from Kristiansand to Oslo was very

Adventures in the Royal Navy, Geoff Barwell.

rough. We had a lifeline along the iron deck in order to get to the radar cabin. One of my shipmates, coming off watch, was very nearly washed overboard. A wave actually threw him at the starboard door leading to the messdeck and he broke his collarbone. For the first time ever my ship had a doctor on board. He was, I believe, a Norwegian doctor taking passage from Kristiansand to Oslo and he was able to look after him. On arrival at Oslo my shipmate was transferred to hospital where, I found out later, he had a wonderful time.

I went ashore for the afternoon and evening on the first day in Oslo. Some of the girls wore headscarves and we learned that their hair had been cut off because they had been fraternising with the enemy.

During the afternoon we met a Norwegian sailor who was serving with the Royal Navy. He had been based in Scotland for most of the war and had just returned to Norway. He was very keen to show us what a lovely country Norway was and how the people had existed since Quisling had taken over the country.

We boarded a train and travelled to the small town of Skien (a forest area where skis were made). We felt quite apprehensive walking around as there were a lot of Germans still there. Some were queuing up at the local picture house with their girlfriends. The scenery was beautiful.

Before we returned to Oslo our Norwegian host invited us into a small cafe. He spoke to two men who produced a sheet of paper as large as a sheet of a newspaper, containing coupons. The lady cafe owner cut the paper by about a quarter and produced about half a dozen rock cakes.

Our host advised us not to eat too many as they were made out of wood pith. When we arrived back at the station to return to Oslo we were invited to have a cup of coffee which turned out to be made of oak leaves. Cigarettes were made out of grass!

Geoffrey Barwell

HMS Vanity *was a 1917 refitted destroyer with a complement of approximately 120. She was engaged mainly on escorting East Coast convoys between Rosyth, Immingham and Sheerness.*
Geoffrey Barwell's sighting of girls who had been humiliated by having their heads shaved must have been a fairly common occurrence after the liberation. They were branded "Tyskerhoren" (German whores). It was estimated that 50,000 Norwegian women had affairs with Germans during the occupation and that 12,000 children were born under the Nazi's "Lebensborn" (fountain of life) project. Relations between German troops and those Norwegian women classed as "true Aryans" were actively encouraged under the puppet regime led by Vidkun Quisling. The children were taken from their mothers and raised as "racially pure" citizens in the Third Reich.

The fleshpots of Malacca

I was with the Army Catering Corps and posted to 45 Regiment, Royal Artillery, at Malacca in 1964. Terendack Camp was on the outskirts of Malacca which was in central Malaysia and some 20 miles from Kuala Lumpur, the nation's capital. The camp covered several square miles and held the army from all nations in various barracks. Terendack was also by the sea and had a beach that you only get in pictures of paradise. On the beach was a NAAFI Club open to all nations.

45 Regt. had its barracks on the right hand side of the main entrance which was very handy when you came back to camp all tanked up after a few Tiger beers, since taxis were not permitted past the main entrance.

On arrival I was introduced to the Staff Sergeant who ran all the messes. He was a man of middle age and portly. He was very friendly and welcomed me to 45 Regt. He introduced me to the other cooks and then showed me where I was to sleep. I had to get ready to see the CO and I was marched into the CO who welcomed me to the Regiment.

I now knew it was to be six or seven weeks before we would go back to Borneo. It was a blessing since what I had been told about Malacca was appealing to my drunken and sexual dreams and ambitions. Having been given the rest of the day off I asked one of the cooks if he fancied a night on the town. He readily agreed to be my guide and show me the places that vicars can only dream about.

Outside the camp main gates there was always a fleet of taxis waiting to take us to Malacca and they always asked us whether we wanted a jigajig or a small boy. "All very clean Johnny."

We found a taxi and asked him to take us to Malacca centre. The driver of the taxi sat facing the passenger door with his feet on the pedals. He would look out of the corner of his eye at where he was going. He would try and sell us his sister for a short time or an all-nighter and, when he came to a bend, which nine times out of ten were blind ones, he would take the opposite side of the road.

In the time I spent in the Far East I'm sure that we were in more danger from the taxi drivers than the enemy.

Finally, we arrived in Malacca with our hearts in our mouths. The taxi driver screeched to a halt at a bar. We paid him his dollar and went into the bar for a Tiger. Being early afternoon there was not much trade about so we were pounced on by the Mamma San as soon as we walked in. We were offered girls. Some of them looked more like an outing from the geriatric hospital and some of them were absolutely gorgeous.

Thanking her politely, we told her "No" We were only in for the beer. We took our drinks over to a table and, as soon as we sat down, a hand appeared at my flies. This girl must have moved with incredible speed as I never even saw it coming.

I took her hand away, more from embarrassment than lack of wanting it to carry full circle, so to speak. We left the bar after downing another of Mamma San's lovely Tiger beers. We wandered around seeing the sights and looking in at some of the shops which sold bargains that made your mind boggle. The prices were so cheap compared to those in the UK. So I bought myself a Seiko watch with an Incabloc movement for twenty dollars which was about £2 sterling. The Incabloc movement meant that every time I moved my wrist or hand the watch would wind itself up. In the UK I would have had to pay around £80 for the same watch.

Having walked around for an age we decided to go for a meal and found ourselves a restaurant. The food was out of this world so we decided to make this our place to bring decent girls who we were trying to impress. After the meal we decided to head back to camp as our money was fast running out.

We found ourselves a taxi and went back to camp. Outside the main gate the taxi dropped us off and we went to one of the bars on the main road, immediately outside the main gate. As well as a bar there were a few shops and a tailor. Out there nobody bought off-the- peg as tailor-made clothes were so cheap. I had a two piece Italian style suit in sharkskin and a pair of hand-made shoes in leather for a tenner. Generally you could pick them up the next day ready to wear.

Ian Read

National Service

Join the Army, learn a trade, adventure, travel - and get paid;
    They're the 'lies' you're fed upon, and like a sucker you sign on.
Then, when they have you in their grip, where are those smiles
- the comradeship?
    Where are those helpful friendly types? Who's the b . . . with the stripes?
Then you're issued with your kit, a uniform that does not fit;
    Brasses left and brasses right, one holdall to be scrubbed snow white.
One belt, the brasses dull and black, one valise and one small pack;
    Pouches basic, buckles 'D', shirts of khaki issue three.
Boots, ammunition, thick with grease - 'aint it ever going to cease?
    Ah! At last, I think he's through. You ask the sergeant what to do.
He looks at you as if you're mad. "You see that kit, *well clean it lad!*"
    This followed by another word, the strangest one you've ever heard.
You look at him with aching heart, but I don't know just where to start;
    The sergeant groans and starts to swear. "You see that b . . . webbing there!
"Well clean it till it looks like new. And you can clean the b. . . . billet too;
    "Then, in the morning, on the dot, I'll be round to inspect the lot!"
And so begins your new career in this unfriendly atmosphere;
    You think of home, you think of bed, sometimes wish that you were dead.
The months roll by. You work - *and how!* Let's look in and see you now;
    Drill parades and kit inspections, brasses bulled to bright perfection.
Weapon training and PT. Life's one endless misery;
    Then, in some dreary office job you count the days to your demob.

How hopeless it appears to you, you find that you have *years* to do!
But then, one day, (don't say I told you) the blokes will say "Hello Old Soldier."
Then you, like me, will feel at peace, because you're nearing your release.
Then you can griff a young lad about the smashing times you've had;
About the service you have seen - and all the places you have been!
Then you say: "Wipe off that frown. Don't let the Army get you down;
"Stick to it lad. Keep smiling through. *I've only got one day to do!"*

I'm not the author of this rhyme. I was stationed at Graz, Austria, from 1951-53 doing National Service with the 1st Battalion, Royal Warwickshire Regiment. I found the poem in an empty locker at the old REME Barracks in Klagenfurt when I attended a course there in 1951. It seemed to me so real, relating to every-day Army life, that I have kept it all those years.

Stan Humphries

The Western Desert

It was not long before we packed up and went by train to Mersa Matruh up in the desert. Here we were equipped with guns, stores and transport and generally prepared for what was to be life in the desert.

It was here at Mersa that I experienced my first sandstorm. It was a case of getting into one's bivouac, getting under a blanket and waiting for it to blow itself out.

We moved out in convoy in a south-westerly direction, our crew riding in the back of a three-ton lorry. We had a canvas cover over us but the back was open, consequently the sand just billowed in as we went along. The flies also came for the ride to add to our discomfort so that, by the end of a day's travelling, it was good to have a brew up and appreciate the cooler evenings.

We slept out by the side of the vehicles, covered by a ground sheet which was always dripping wet with dew by morning. Our daily ration of water did not permit much in the way of washing. The more one drank the more one sweated so that the swirling sand in the convoy caked more readily on one's person.

It was quite a relief when we reached the oasis of Siwa where we set up the gun site to prepare for any hostile air activity. It was an interesting place with a large well in the middle of the village.

The local inhabitants regarded us with great suspicion from their cave dwellings cut into the hillside. Fresh dates from the palm trees were a most welcome addition to our diet and it was good to get cleaned up a bit with a plentiful supply of water. We did not see much action, but fired a few rounds at an occasional JU88 but did not come under any serious attack.

Then we set off in convoy to the west, calling at the oasis of Jarabub before turning north following the frontier barbed-wire boundary running between Egypt and Libya. This was a rather remarkable frontier, the barbed wire fence being several feet wide and running for mile after mile from north to south.

By this time the 8th Army was pushing westwards towards Tobruk to relieve the garrison after it had been besieged for several months. It was in the middle of December 1941 when we formed up just outside Tobruk and went in two or three days before Christmas.

Fred Frost

Harsh Korean winter

All the Korean houses *(in a POW camp)* were heated with a counter-sunk kitchen at one end. Here was the wood fire and the smoke and the heat passed under the other two rooms to the chimney at the other end.

It was a unique system that worked well as long as fires were not allowed to get too big. Then the first floor nearest the fire became unbearable. In the particularly bad winter of 1952-53 the frost would be on the inside walls and the covers on top of us would sometimes be stiff with frost.

Nevertheless, we all remained as we lay - head to foot on the hot floor.

The winters in North Korea were very harsh. At night the temperature was 40 below and all the rivers and streams were frozen solid.

The days and nights passed slower than ever and the truce talks dragged on and on. Most nights were lengthened as the bombers droned overhead, then the Chinese switched the feeble lights off and we were left in the darkness till dawn.

Each dawn we were roused from our huts for roll call, the tannoy system around the camp usually blared forth Chinese or Russian martial music. But we were often greeted by the strong voice of Paul Robson singing "Arise, ye prisoners of starvation, arise ye wretched of the earth."

Then, platoon by platoon, we paraded down the main street to the town square around the Red Star Monument and back again. Our faces were frozen and blue with cold.

Henry O'Kane

Pre-Yalta confab

On entering Grand Harbour, Valetta (aboard *HMS Orion*,) we tied up in Dockyard Creek alongside the sunken oil tanker *Ohio* , its bridge being level with our quarterdeck.

Imagine our surprise when Winston Churchill came on board accompanied by his daughter Sarah, apparently to stay for a few days.

Another surprise was when an American warship tied up alongside the same quay just ahead of us. They immediately started building a most elaborate gangway, about six feet wide, with a very gradual slope down to the quay. Then the buzz went round that President Roosevelt was on board and that the special gangway was for him to come down in his wheelchair.

Coming off watch the following day the Captain of Marines asked me to deliver an invitation to the American Marine Captain inviting him to dinner that evening.

I left the ship by the forward gangway. As I did so a woman in a smart khaki green outfit walked past along the quay. I followed some yards behind.

As we approached the gangway of the American ship she slowed down as if expecting me to pass. I thought "ladies first", so she started up the gangway. The sentry at the bottom presented arms. I followed at a discreet distance, but the sentry remained at the present until I had passed as well.

When I reached the top there was President Roosevelt surrounded by dozens of officers, a military band and a guard of honour. The President was sitting in his wheelchair a few feet away from me.

Immediately I was confronted by two large plain clothes men, each of whom had one hand tucked ominously inside their jackets. When I told them who I was they came out with that immortal phrase: *"Get to hell out of here!"*

John Curtis

Unknown to John Curtis, Churchill and Roosevelt were having a secret confab at Malta to work out their strategy before meeting Stalin at the Yalta Conference in the Crimea, from February 4 to 11, 1945, at which the three decided how they would carve up post-war Germany and Poland. In his memoirs Churchill describes how he flew from Northolt on January 29, 1945, together with his daughter Sarah.

"I took up my quarters on HMS Orion *where I rested all day. In the evening I felt better and both the Governor of Malta and Mr Harriman dined with me."*

"On the morning of February 2 the Presidential party, on board the USS Quincy, *steamed into Valetta harbour. It was a warm day and under a cloudless sky I watched the scene from the deck of the* Orion. *As the American cruiser steamed slowly past us towards her berth alongside the quay I could see the figure of the President, seated on the bridge, and we waved to each other."*

"With the escort of Spitfires overhead, the salutes and the bands of the ships' companies in the harbour playing "The Star-spangled Banner" it was a splendid scene."

Roosevelt, aged 63, died on April 12, 1945, little more than five weeks after the incident described by John Curtis.

The sweat box

The Bridge on the River Kwai with Alec Guinness is now part of WW2 folklore, especially the cruelty of the Japanese. Remember the "sweatbox" in which Guinness was imprisoned?

I know how he felt.

Imagine a steel box, inside a steel watertight compartment, inside a steel ship. The outside temperature is 110 degrees F. The steel deck would burn your feet - or fry an egg. Even with hatches open and an awning erected, sitting at anchor in harbour was like living in an oven.

No. We did not have air conditioning. No. We did not have air coolers. No. We did not have any air circulating fans. But we *did* have a heating system! We had gone out east from the Home Fleet at Scapa with no time to collect cooling equipment (if it ever existed). We did, however, have some white shorts and sleeveless shirts.

But back to that steel box. . . .

Ships, like cars, require maintenance. The steel box contained switch gear which was operated by remote control from a central switchboard to isolate sections of the ship into independent sections in case of damage.

Maintenance meant opening the compartment and letting the watertight door stay open for two hours in the hope that it would cool down. The lid on the switch box was a steel plate, some 60 lbs in weight, with 24 steel bolts holding it in position. The watertight seal consisted of asbestos string around the bolts sunk into a fireproof putty.

The 24 bolts had to be removed, the steel plate removed, the surfaces cleaned of old string and putty, the switchgear serviced, a new joint created on the edge of the box, the plate replaced and bolted in position. Then, through a separate screw hole, the air had to be sucked out to create a vacuum pressure which must not drop for 20 minutes, proving the watertight joint.

It was a simple straightforward maintenance job . . . except for the intense heat.

Working dress for the job was a pair of open sandals, with a leather sole to stop the feet burning, and a pair of swimming trunks.

The Maintenance Engineer - myself - had a mate who was an experienced torpedo man. He would tie a string around my leg and then stand outside the compartment watching the clock for a maximum of two minutes. Then he would pull the string. If I did not come out in five seconds then he would come and get me out. Every second did count.

This was followed by a minimum of five minutes rest sipping lime juice, preferably in the fresh air. The it was back for two minutes more, repeating the procedure until the job was finished.

As I stepped into the compartment the pores of my skin went pop! Perspiration ran in streams from every pore in my body, off my chin, my elbows, my hands, down my body to my legs; within seconds I was awash with sweat. Just try to exert pressure on a spanner to unscrew a bolt with wet hands. Even worse, tightening them up again.

The Royal Navy recognised the difficulty of the job by paying me "danger money". They paid me an extra twenty eight bob per week *(£1.40)* on top of my pay for the period of the work. Having joined up at a fighting weight of 11 stone, I dropped to seven and a half before they sent me to a rest camp to recuperate.

Alex Guinness never had the five minute breaks, nor the lime juice. Then again, he was a prisoner of a cruel enemy. I was just a volunteer in the Royal Navy. The MO said the lime juice was to cool my blood and stop it from overheating. I think he thought I was a robot.

The irony was that 70 air circulating fans arrived by cargo ship on the day that we were recalled to the home Fleet.

Norman Schofield

An eventful desert journey

It was in May 1942 that I was informed that I was being sent on a gunnery instructors' course at Haifa, where the Middle East training depot was located.

I had only a vague idea of where Haifa was, whereupon I was informed that it was up the coast in what was then Palestine. How to get there presented me with the feeling that I was entering into the unknown.

The time came for me to pack my kit, collect a travel warrant and board the ration truck which was going into Tobruk. It was considered that my best bet was to get on to the coast road and get a lift to the rail head at Capuzzo, about 90 miles away, where I should board the train to Cairo and, from there, another train via Tel Aviv to Haifa.

Fortunately the ration truck dropped me off near a Military Police checkpoint where a 15 cwt. truck was stopped on it way to Capuzzo. So I climbed in the back and went on my way. It was an open truck, the sun was hot, and the dust swirled round in a choking cloud.

It was always wise to keep a lookout at the sky above ready to do a quick dive over the side in the event of a visit by German ME 109 fighter planes which had a habit of strafing the one and only road along the coast.

Eventually I arrived at the railhead without any bother.

This was where the railway line just stopped in the desert with nothing more pretentious than a set of buffers.

About 200 yards away there was a cookhouse where I managed to join fellow travellers for the usual bully beef stew and a very welcome mug of tea. Accommodation for the night was basic but practical. I wandered about until I found a slit trench, dropped in with my kit, covered myself with my ground sheet and tried to get some sleep.

It was still dark when we were roused to go to the cookhouse for porridge, tinned bacon and tea, after which I managed to find my slit trench, collect my kit, and set off with the others to board the train.

It consisted of a line of goods wagons with sliding doors along the sides through which we had to climb. The trucks were unusual in that they had jagged holes in the sides and roof, the result, I was told, of the attention of the German ME 109s which usually met this train somewhere en route when crossing the desert.

There was a flat topped wagon on each end of the train manned by New Zealanders with their Bofers anti-aircraft guns.

There were only two of us in one of the wagons, so we had plenty of room to spread out by the wide open doors. With much clanging and banging our engine attached itself to the front of the train and we set off into the desert as the first streaks of dawn came up over the horizon.

For mile after mile we rattled our way across a great expanse of nothing but sand and scrub until it suddenly happened . . .

There was a tremendous crashing and banging as the engine driver slammed on the brakes and the whole line of wagons came together one behind the other. We did not wait to discover what had happened . We dived out through the opening, rolling over in the sand at the side of the track. The two German fighter planes which had strafed the length of the train were climbing and banking then turning to come in for another run.

This time the engine went up in a cloud of steam and a few more ventilation holes were made in the wagons. While we were getting as far away from the track as possible and flattening ourselves in the sand we were quite relieved to see two RAF Hurricanes appear and chase the Messerschmidts over the horizon.

There was quite a long wait before another engine reached the scene to take us on our way.

Cairo was reached that evening and I stayed overnight at the small hotel I had used when on leave earlier. The next day I reported to the RTO at the railway station and joined the crowd of various nationalities to await the arrival of the train to Haifa. The gates allowing passengers on to the platform were not opened until the train drew in.

Unfortunately for those of us waiting towards the rear of the train, our gate was never opened. Crowds just fought their way through the gate towards the front of the train until all the carriages were packed. Then off it went leaving crowds still standing there.

I was informed that the next train left at the same time on the following day. I was fortunate having an extra day in Cairo, but made sure I was in front at the right gate next day.

The transformation on the journey, from desert to beautifully cultivated fields, orange groves, and farms was quite incredible. It was a different world.

The remainder of the journey was uneventful. The fact that I had arrived a day late for the course was not unexpected.

Fred Frost

Faraway places... and strange-sounding names

On November 8, 1939, I volunteered for the Navy and was told to go home and await my call-up which was in February 1940 and to tell them that I had "volunteered for the Navy." I awaited a medical in June and the outcome was A2 for the Navy and A1 for the Army! So I decided on the Royal Artillery since I had a pal in that branch of the Service.

I was given a warrant to report to Fullwood Barracks, **Preston**, on June 19 and, after a meal and a train journey with armed sentries, finished up at **Stranraer** and then by ship to Larne, Northern Ireland, and **Dundrum**, Co. Down.

I was sent to 17th ITC Royal Irish Fusiliers at **Ballykinlar** Camp which was known as "world's end camp" - and it seemed like it.

After recruit training I was appointed u/p (unpaid) L/Cpl and told by the CO that my orders would be supported by all Officers and NCOs. But, after six months, I went to **Belfast** for eye tests and, unknown to me, was downgraded to B7 (or something) and was transferred to a Home Battalion (5th RIF) for the defence of Northern Ireland. I spent time on detachments guarding telephone exchanges, ammunition dumps, petrol points etc. After two years we were made up into a service battalion.

Meanwhile I had been regraded A1 and had volunteered for the Palestine Police, the Royal West African Frontier Force and the RAF, to no avail.

After another year, and one or two cadres in a battle school, together with a pay duties course, I became Intelligence Sergeant. From August 1942, while I was in Armagh on a cipher course (low grade) I had to decode and encode messages from and to our CO.

In June 1943 we were to be disbanded and sent to other formations. I was sent to 7th RUR at **Saltfleet, Lincs.**, where I met my brother who was with the RAF at Manby. A fortnight at **Welbeck Abbey**, training with tanks in **Sherwood Forest**, was followed by another Battle School course at **Catterick**.

I was seconded to the Royal West African Frontier Force and sailed from **Liverpool**, pulled into **Gibraltar**, took a dash in our ship the *SS Orbita* to **Casablanca**, then to **Freetown**, and from there, in a smaller French ship *SS Thysville* to **Takoradi-Cumasi, Gold Coast (Ghana)**, to **Accra (via Kunesi)** and on to **Teshi (Ghana)**.

After some months there we sailed again through the Mediterranean to **Alexandria** and then via the **Suez Canal** and **Red Sea**, on a Dutch ship the *SS Sibajak* to **Dakar, Senegal**. Then to **Aden**, to refuel, and across the **Indian Ocean** to **Bombay**; by train to **Dhone (Deecan)** to await further instructions.

While I was there the first person I met came from my own village so we exchanged a few yarns over a few beers.

A few months later it was on again to **Calcutta** and, after a short while, on again to **Dhozari** and **Comilla (Bangladesh)**, then by train up to the **Bramhaputra** and into **Assam**.

14

From Comilla I took a "khistie" (dug out) back up the **River Sangu** to join up with the 1st Battalion Gambia Regiment , Royal West African Frontier Force, where I took over as Orderly Room Sergeant.

Then, again up river to **Ruma** and **Mowdock, Frontier Hill**, and down into **Burma**. Then I travelled down through Burma along the **Kaladan Valley**, across the River Kaladan, to just outside **Buthidaung** where I was evacuated with bronchitis to hospital in **Cox's Bazar**. I rejoined the Battalion, now withdrawn to **Cheringha** for a few weeks.

Then it was to **Chittagong (Bangladesh),** and over to **Madras** via the *SS Nevassa*. From Madras I went up country to a village called **Khavetenarga**. In the surrounding area the 81st West Africa Division had spent over 18 months in contact with the enemy, the longest of any unit in the war.

After a trip to **Bangalore** and a spell in **Mysore State** I was told to go home on leave to the UK!

I set off to **Doelali** and, while there, I heard that the Japanese had given in following two atom bombs. We hung around for a few weeks and then set off for **Karach**i via **Delhi** and **Lahore**.

There we took off for **Bahrain, Habania (Baghdad)**; **Lydda (Israel)**; **El Adam (Tobruk)**, to **Sardinia** and, from there, to **Taunton** in the UK and **London**.

After leave I took a train to **Waterbeach (Cambs.)** and travelled in the bomb bay of a Liberator to **Tripoli**. But, owing to a storm over the Mediterranean, we turned back to **Marseilles**. After three days we got to **Tripoli** and, from there, to **Cairo** and stayed by the **Pyramids** and **Sphinx**. From there it was to **Karachi, Poona**, and **Madras** and then to join the Battalion - only to learn that they were preparing to go back to **West Africa**.

I was promoted to C/Sgt. (CQMS) of HQ Company. and went off to **Cochin, India,** to embark on the *Empire Pride* to sail back the way we came to **Bathhurst (now Banjul)** where we off loaded our Africans and demobbed them.

We Europeans were entertained by the locals before setting off for **Freetown** where the *Highland Princess* was waiting to take the Europeans home. But I opted to stay on in Freetown for personal reasons in connection with my rank. I stayed a month with two others and we demobbed some more Africans and then went down to the docks to board the *SS Sobieski*, a Polish boat, en route to the UK via the **Azores** to pick up RAF personnel.

I returned to **Liverpool** where I had first set out. On June 9, 1946, six years after joining up, I was placed on the "A" Reserve.

It was more like a Cooks Tour and, on looking back, I regard it as the best days of my life. I was fortunate only suffering small spells in hospital, not through injury, but with dysentery and bronchitis.

Wilfred George Pincham.

Chapter 2

Under attack

When war begins, then hell openeth.
GEORGE HERBERT (1593-1633)

In the Air, 1942

I left England on August 12, 1942, *(in a Halifax bomber as part of the First Pathfinder Squadron)* and we were hit heavily by flack over Le Havre while being coned by searchlights for two or three minutes. When we approached Le Havre to bomb a German raider in the docks, I was the air bomber in charge of the operation.

Our squadron leader was a stickler for photographs of each aircraft's bomb burst and every effort was made to comply with his directions.

On this Le Havre operation I had told Mick (our engineer and least experienced member of the crew) to release the photo flare immediately after I had shouted "bombs gone." While I was waiting to see the strikes it was obvious that either no flare had been dispatched or, if it had, it was faulty and had not ignited.

Therefore I told the skipper to go round again and yelled at Mick to send off another flare through the chute when I gave the word. Meanwhile we were receiving a battering from heavy anti-aircraft fire.

We were being thrown about and hit by countless numbers of small metal fragments. The sound was similar to gravel being thrown on a tin roof.

It was when we were doing this second run over the target that we were holed quite badly near the mid upper gun turret. Unfortunately the shell burst severed vital aircraft control wires and we were unable to steer a course.

Later, at the first opportunity, I asked Mick why he did not have a flare at the time of bombing. I was unable to get a satisfactory explanation except that he failed to release the flare. I came to the conclusion that he simply "froze" when we were under attack and failed to do his duty. It was his first operation but this does not excuse his conduct.

At the skipper's command *"abandon aircraft!"* we unplugged oxygen, intercom, and fastened parachutes. Then I opened up the escape hatch and dispatched all except the pilot. I had to stamp on Jimmy Reynolds fingers to make him release his grip on the aircraft and let himself fall.

When all were out I checked the pilot's harness and parachute, freed him from the intercom and oxygen, asked him if he was in control and received the affirmative. Then I clipped on my parachute and jumped.

All this was accomplished in about one minute during which we were travelling in a predominantly southerly direction and losing height.

We all bailed out over the sea, but drifted on to the coast in the vicinity of

Honfleur. Shortly after 3 am we all landed in the neighbourhood of Honfleur and were eventually captured and later taken to Le Havre in an American truck!

Eric Herwin

At Sea, 1944.

"Enemy aircraft - low level at Green 45. Expect torpedo bombers,

"High level aircraft at Red 30 - be prepared for Kamikaze,

"Low flying enemy aircraft at Red 70,

"Further aircraft at high level - Green 55,

. . . Fire at Will!"

Feelings. Exciting? It depends on your point of view! It's certainly OK on the cinema or television screen. But . . .

When these words are coming over a tannoy, you are closed up at action stations on a British battle cruiser *(HMS Renown)* in the Indian ocean, with all secondary armament banging away like hell on earth, and especially when your station is damage control, then it's not so much exciting as bloody terrifying!

Damage Control Station. Damage Control Station meant dressing in asbestos clothing and wearing a tin hat. In my case, as an electrical mechanic, it meant lying on the armoured deck (four inches of hardened and thick steel) and fore and aft watertight bulkhead doors had been closed, sectionalising the ship. The floor hatch led to a shaft down thirty feet to a generator where another kindred spirit had just been entombed by me closing the hatch.

The job. The job was to repair any damage created by enemy action within my section, to maintain the ship as a fighting unit, keep open lines of communication from the bridge to the bilges, from fore to aft.

A hive of activity? No sir. Total *inactivity*! With hands over tin helmet protecting the head, with your brain turning over the drills and routines that have been practised for torpedo strikes, shell bursts, direct bomb hits... only this time it was for real.

The brain could not stop recalling our sister ship the *Repulse* which, together with the *Prince of Wales*, was lost to those same Japs in somewhat similar circumstances.

The situation. We were not alone. We were, in fact, the Flag Ship of the Eastern Fleet, flying the flag of Admiral Powers. We had just paid a visit to Sabang where, on April 18, 1944, 70 planes from our American and British aircraft carriers had destroyed three of the four major oil tanks and bombed the harbour and the airport.

During our air battle *Renown* fired 700 rounds of 4.5 inch ammunition in 30 minutes; six of the bombers were shot down. On this occasion no ships were hit.

In retrospect, a successful mission but at that moment I aged twelve months.

Norman Schofield

On the Ground, 1964

On one patrol *(in Borneo)* we lay in wait along a jungle track for three days after intelligence told us that a patrol of Indonesians was coming to attempt to capture our guns. There were 12 of us positioned at intervals along the track. The Gurkhas were further down the route and the idea was to trap the enemy in an ambush between the two groups. It was the monsoon season and we were soaked through. We were beginning to get fed up and were prepared to call it a day when we heard a movement further down the track.

Some raw recruits, straight from a three-day jungle training course, were in our group and this was the first time they had been on patrol.

The method of ambush was to let the enemy get level along the path and then open fire. But one of the recruits panicked and fired a fraction too quickly. All hell was let loose and seven of our side were killed and two badly wounded.

Fortunately the Gurkhas came to the rescue and most of the enemy were killed. The rest fled when the air support which we had frantically called up by radio came in. We were picked up by helicopter and taken back to barracks and debriefed.

I don't blame the man who fired too soon. It is the sort of thing that could happen to anyone. But it was an unnerving experience. I got a few scratches in the encounter but it left me with mental scars. For a long time I got flash-backs to that day and it happens even now if I am low or depressed. I get a feeling of guilt. I don't know why.

Certainly my outlook on life altered that day - and I regard every day as precious!

Ian Read

During operations in Borneo, 1962-66, the British Forces lost 16 dead.

Chapter 3

Target for Tonight

One enemy is too many,
And a hundred friends too few.
GERMAN PROVERB

50 years after the event a pilot discovered he had
crippled a U-boat - and met the crew

Flt. Lieutenant John Whiteley, the pilot of a Lancaster bomber, was sent on
a mission to bomb the German light cruiser Koln *in a Norwegian fjord in*
December 1944. The RAF crew failed to find the target. Instead they bombed
what they thought was enemy merchant shipping. Fifty years later the pilot
was amazed to discover from his former enemies that he had unwittingly
bombed a German U-boat, putting it out of action. The U-boat crew, who
survived his attack, invited him to be guest of honour at their reunion.

Although they are not entirely commonplace reunions between wartime
antagonists sometimes do take place. While it is entirely understandable that
members of similar formations seek out each other, it is more improbable that those
who fought in entirely different environments would get together. That members of
a U-boat crew should seek out members of Bomber Command for a reunion must
border on the unique, especially when the bomber crew which attacked the U-boat
were unaware of its presence.

My story begins on the night of December 28-29 December, 1944 and arises
from an operation on the Oslo Fjord by No 5 Group, Bomber Command, when U-
boat 682 happened to be on the receiving end of some rather unpleasant visiting
cards. That night I was pilot of 619 Squadron Lancaster PG-H which was one of 68
Lancasters which took part in the operation.

Until I received the Squadron Association Bulletin for September 1993, I had
given little thought to the operation. I think I regarded it as one more operation to
my tour of 30 operations.

In the Bulletin the Squadron Association Secretary wrote that he had received
some very strange requests, but none as strange as one from the South East RAF
Association, enclosing a letter from the former Bo'sun of U-boat 682 which had
been at the end of a somewhat unsuccessful Bomber Command raid on the
Norwegian fjord at Horten. It was a request for any of the RAF crew to get in touch
and perhaps join one of the reunions which were held at regular intervals.

The Bulletin mentioned that five crews from 619 Squadron took part in the
operation, and they included John Whiteley. If they, or anybody else, would be

interested the Secretary promised to send details. I was curious to know more about Herr Wodarz's invitation. It would appear that the Bo'sun had written initially to the United States records office because the Germans were under the impression that the Americans had been involved in the Oslo Fjord raid. As the United States did not carry out night operations they were eliminated. It was established that the real culprits were No 5 Group, Bomber Command.

Before the Oslo Fjord raid I was based at Strubby, a Bomber Command airfield five miles south west of Mablethorpe, a small seaside resort on the Lincolnshire coast. In my tour of 30 operations I can recall some vividly. Other operations are now a vague memory. I have, however, a reasonably fair recollection of the Oslo Fjord operation.

About 1000 hrs. I was told by my flight commander that my crew, together with four others from 619 Squadron, had been selected for an operation that night. On the display board I was shown the battle order and the five crews who were to operate that night. Of the five only three crews survived the war.

My immediate task was to collect my crew and to get to Lancaster PG-H and carry out the usual pre-flight tests and make sure the aircraft was airworthy. In the meantime the bowser crew had been instructed to fill the Lancaster with 1,800 gallons of fuel. Armourers had been told to bomb up with 14 x 1,000 lb. armour piercing bombs.

While this was taking place we had no knowledge of the target. Bearing in mind the fuel load, I had estimated an operation of between six and seven hours. I also surmised from the type of bombs we were carrying and the limited number of Squadron aircraft which were being used, it was going to be a special operation.

The five crews reported to the operations room at 1500 hrs when the Station Commander pulled back a curtain which was covering a large wall map to reveal the target. He explained the reason for the operation which was to comprise 68 Lancasters.

He was followed by the Squadron Commander who confirmed the fuel and bomb loads and pointed out the routes to and from the target and gave us the time of take off and the time over the Oslo Fjord. Next to speak was the Intelligence Officer whose brief was somewhat scanty. He could tell us little about the German flack, searchlights, or the possible presence of German night fighters. Lastly, the Meteorological Officer indicated the likely weather to and from Norway and the Oslo Fjord. On this occasion he got it just about right, but I have to say that in those days the Met forecast could be notoriously inaccurate.

We were informed that the primary target was the German light cruiser *Koln* which was believed to be in the Oslo Fjord, but its exact position was unknown. We were informed that the Royal Navy was very anxious that Bomber Command should put this ship out of action to eliminate its menacing presence in the Atlantic. If the *Koln* could not be located the second target was to be German merchant shipping.

Until I received my Squadron Association Bulletin for September 1993, I had no idea that U-boats were present in the Oslo Fjord, and this is confirmed by the debriefing reports of the crew in the Squadron operations book.

I took off at 1950 hrs. on December 28 in Lancaster PG-H. I flew on a course of roughly zero-four-five at a height of 1,000 feet above the North Sea in order not to be picked up by German radar until we had almost reached Norway. About ten minutes before we arrived at the southern end of the fjord I started a rapid climb at 1,000 ft. a minute to an operational height of 7,500 ft. The next 25 minutes were spent in speeding up and down the fjord looking for the *Koln* but without success.

As we passed Horten, on our port side about 40 miles south of Oslo, it was quite apparent from the none too friendly reception which we received there was German shipping in the harbour.

The reason for our failure to find the *Koln* will become clear when I tell you about my meeting with Sven Thienemann the Captain of U-boat 682. Since we had been unable to locate the *Koln* I ordered my bomb aimer to align our Lancaster up on German merchant shipping which was tied up in the port of Horten. He said he spotted a ship and gave me instructions and brought the aircraft up into the correct bombing position. We dropped half our bomb load from a height of 7,500 ft. at 2348 hrs. We passed over Horten and I then turned the Lancaster round to roughly a reciprocal heading for the second run up. My bomb aimer lined up on another ship and we released the remaining bombs at 2354 hrs.

After we had secured our second photograph my immediate task was to get away from Horten as quickly as possible as the Germans were being distinctly unfriendly. Jim Garrett, my Australian navigator, gave me a course to fly back to base. I rapidly lost height down to 1,000 ft. heading for Strubby and landed at 0230 hrs. on December 29, 1944. We had been airborne for 6 hours 40 minutes.

It was always a great relief to be back at the dispersal point after an operation and I carried out my usual inspection of the aircraft to see if it had sustained any damage. I am glad to tell you that on this occasion we had come through unscathed. It was then a case of waiting for transport to take us back for debriefing. For the Horton operation I particularly remember my crew and I were debriefed by a newly commissioned WAAF Officer.

They would put the usual questions to us: "What were the weather conditions like to and from the target area?" "Did we see any German fighters?" "Was there much flack?" "Were there any searchlights?" "What was the height at which we bombed?" "What were the times at which we bombed?" "Had we seen any aircraft shot down?"

As the debriefing continued the WAAF Officer was becoming very tiresome by continuing to ask questions like: "Why were you not able to find the *Koln*?" "Did you make a thorough search of the fjord?"

Bearing in mind that the time was now after 0300 hrs. and remembering I had been strapped in the pilot's seat for 30 minutes before take off and for 15 minutes after landing and having flown the Lancaster for 6 hours 40 minutes (like many pilots I never used the automatic pilot) I was feeling rather irritable and hungry.

Then the Intelligence Officer asked John Hurst, my bomb aimer, if he could tell her the number of masts on each ship we had bombed at Horten! His reply was something like this: "Madam! If we had been flying 100 ft. lower I could have given you the ruddy *name* of the ship!"

This was just one example of the trials and tribulations of the bomber crew at debriefing.

Having given a resume of the Horten operation in 1944 I can now take up the story 50 years on . . .

There was this invitation to the crew which had participated in the raid to join Herr Herbert Wodarz, and the crew of the U-boat 682 at their reunion which was taking place in May 1994. I wrote and said that my wife and I would be happy to come to Germany and meet him and his colleagues. The last time I had been to Germany was in May 1946 as Captain of a DC3 Dakota flying to the headquarters of the British Air Force of Occupation. For my wife it was her first visit.

The thought of meeting my enemy of 50 years ago aroused a measure of apprehension, curiosity and excitement. I was very pleased when I heard that Ken Hickmott and Ken Phillips, two old colleagues from 619 Squadron, who had also taken part in the Oslo Fjord operation, were joining the reunion. We made it to the small town of Zeltingen-Rachtig on the River Mosel, about 60 miles south of Koblenz to be the guests of U-boat 682.

We met our German hosts and joined them for dinner. Any lingering doubts we had were immediately dispersed by Herr Sven Thienemann, the Captain of U-boat 682, an upright and sprightly man whose 82 years completely belied his age. In perfect English he introduced himself and his wife to us. We were invited to sit at their table for dinner.

The ice having been broken the former enemies quickly became friends.

Sven Thienemann told me he had joined the German merchant navy in 1929 at the age of 17. He had sailed round Cape Horn three times under sail and had visited England on numerous occasions pre-war. He had also been Captain of the Onassis yacht.

During our reunion Sven showed us a chart of the German naval positions during the raid. He pointed out that the *Koln* had been secreted in a small inlet on the Swedish side of the Oslo Fjord and it was most unlikely to have been seen from a height of 7,500 ft. This explained why the Lancaster crews were unable to find the German light cruiser.

Incidentally, the *Koln* left Norway on January 9, 1945 and sailed to Wilhelmshaven where it was sunk by bomber Command on March 31, 1945.

U-boat 682 had been so severely damaged in the Horten operation that it was still out of action when the war ended. It never went to sea again and it was cannibalised for spare parts. Fortunately none of the crew was injured by our bombs.

I was, however, surprised to learn that No 5 Group had sunk U-boat 735 and the sole survivor of that bombing was Herbert Hermann who had joined the reunion together with his wife. I have to say there was a moment's hesitation when I was introduced to him. But old scores can be quickly forgiven although even more than 50 years on they can never be forgotten. Mutual respect between former enemies developed during that reunion and, more important, new friendships were forged.

Since our first visit we have attended their reunions in subsequent years.

John Whiteley

All is forgiven. Lancaster pilot John Whiteley (left) met up with U-boat Captain Sven Thienemann in May 1997 and learned how, 50 years earlier, he had unwittingly hit an enemy submarine.

Chapter 4

Just Fancy That!

What's the use of worrying. It never was worth while.
GEORGE ASAF (1915) - (PACK UP YOUR TROUBLES IN YOUR OLD KIT BAG...)

A 'dangerous' posting

After commissioning I went to the 5th Bn., Manchester Regiment (TA) and went home on seven days leave with instructions to report to some place in Wiltshire where the Battalion was stationed.

In the middle of my leave I received a telegram to report to the RTO at Aberdeen Station as part of "Force K". Vague disturbing thoughts floated through my mind of Aberdeen being the nearest major port to Norway and I thought we might be on our way there. On arrival, together with another friend, I found I was on my way to Balmoral Castle where our Battalion was the first English regiment to provide security for the Royal Family.

We were very comfortably settled in what had been a lumber camp built by Canadian troops who were cutting down some of the pine forests. We had loads of wood for the very efficient Canadian wood burning stoves and we were very comfortable. Duty consisted of patrolling the banks of the River Dee to prevent attack, particularly by parachutists.

This went on night and day, but our peaceful life persisted; 24 hours on guard, 24 hours on reserve; 24 hours training, mainly mountain climbing and running.

John Carmichael, a Birmingham policeman who had hair-raising experiences during the blitz, became a soldier. But he considered his most dangerous mission was the occasion he had to partner the Queen Mother at a dance.

Royal Inspection at Balmoral Castle. John Carmichael stands rigidly to attention on the right of the picture.

On these runs we often encountered Queen Elizabeth (the Queen Mother) in her pony and trap accompanied by the two Princesses. Princess Elizabeth would be about 17 and Princess Margaret about 14. When we met them we always stopped, as did the Queen, and she had some very informal chats with members of the platoon: Where did they come from? Any family? I think the lads appreciated these talks. It was something to tell their families about much later - not in their letters which, at that time and because of our situation, were censored by junior officers like me. It was a job I hated.

I paid several visits to the famous Crathie Church for morning services with the Royal Family and the local people. After Church the King and Queen and all members of the family came back to the Officers' Mess for sherry. One evening, surprisingly, they attended a camp concert which I think they enjoyed. We, being a Lancashire Regiment, based at Wigan in peacetime, had quite a few budding comedians and singers.

Towards the end of our stay the famous Ghillies' (gamekeepers) Ball was held at the Castle and all available officers and the members of the Regimental Concert Party were invited to be present.

What a memorable occasion it was! After assembling in a beautiful anti-room we were introduced individually to King George and Queen Elizabeth and the Princesses. I always remember it was like a scene from a film set. You descended into the ballroom by a red carpeted double staircase.

The highlight of my evening - and probably the most dangerous part of my army service - was just about to arrive. The adjutant warned me that I would be partnering the Queen in the dance after next!

It was a Scottish Country Dance!

All my fears were unfounded, although I remained in a bit of a tizzy. She was delightful. Her first words: "I know from your accent that you are a Scot like me." She never let the conversation flag, enquiring about my home, my wife, children (none at that time), my job, about Birmingham which she had visited twice during the blitz period.

What a delightful dancer. She was like a fairy.

What she thought of my dancing went unrecorded.

John Carmichael

Downside up

Either in 1942 or early 1943 I was with a party ammunitioning a ship when a young S/Lieut. RNVR asked me if I was i/c loading. On confirmation that I was, he handed me an important Admiralty Instruction or AFO (Admiralty Fleet Order). I kept a copy, part of which reads:

It is necessary for technical reasons that these warheads should be stored with the top at the bottom and the bottom at the top. In order that there may be no doubt as to which is the top and which is the bottom for storage purposes, it will be seen that the bottom has been plainly labelled with the word 'TOP'.

Donald Ferguson

The fair way

During the Gulf War the most heavily guarded airfield in the world was Dhahran in Saudi Arabia.

I had promised to take a visitor, a high-ranking civilian official from the Ministry of Defence, to the airfield to catch the flight back to Brize Norton. Without even checking my identity or searching the civilian staff car the Saudi Army guard started to wave me through because I was in uniform. He was about to raise the barrier when he spotted the civilian passenger. The soldier insisted on seeing his pass. He had none.

I managed to contact the Saudi officer in charge but the answer was unequivocal: "No pass - no enter."

We tried different entrances with the same result. I could see the Tristar on the runway with the RAF crew waiting for the VIP. It was a tantalising 700 metres away, but totally unapproachable.

"Don't you have anything at all?" I asked in desperation.

"Absolutely nothing. I came away in such a tearing hurry," said the VIP searching through his wallet and producing his Visa card.

"No good. They only take bribes in cash." I tried to sound cheerful, but I felt terribly responsible.

"I've nothing but the card for my golf club," he said still searching hidden flaps in the wallet. Absolutely splendid! It carried his photograph!

We showed it to the guard who made a great show of checking the identity and comparing the picture with my civilian passenger. He made a feeble effort at what might have been an attempt to present arms and we drove on to the airfield and parked alongside the Tristar with minutes to spare. The RAF crew were as relieved as I was.

Aubrey Chalmers

The thunder box

One of the more amusing incidents of my service (with the Queen's Regiment) occurred during a six month tour of Belize on the Guatemala-Mexico border in 1977.

One of our duties was to man an observation post, known as Cadenaus OP, on the top of a hill on the border of Belize and Guatemala. There were only two ways to reach the post: by helicopter or, for the more adventurous, by assault boat along the River Sarstoon, followed by a nice hike through the jungle up a steep track winding between trees with six-inch spikes protruding from them. When the ground was slippery and your natural instinct was to grab the first thing which came within reach to save yourself, gloves and/or a good supply of plasters was a must.

The OP in question looked over the border towards Guatemala at a new military camp which was being built. The accommodation was sunk into the ground and made from sandbag walls with a corrugated iron roof. As the height inside was less than five feet, and we spent up to ten days at a time in the OP, a lot of crouching and backache ensued.

The latrine at the OP was on a jetty sticking out from the side of the mountain and consisted of a "thunder box" with four six-foot stakes supporting a wooden roof and hessian sides. One of the duties at the end of each day was to throw about a cup of helicopter fuel (we used to call it "nev gas") down the thunder box and then throw a lighted match down to burn off the fumes and the germs.

One evening, while we were enjoying watching the sunset over the mountains, one of the section was sent to clean the latrine. I noticed him pass by with what looked like a full can of "nev gas" and return a few minutes later with the can looking much lighter - almost empty in fact!

My suspicions were confirmed by my companions, closely followed by our chorus of *"No Dave . . . Stop!"*

But it was too late.

There was a tremendous explosion followed by a 20 foot high flame which illuminated the area for miles around. The explosion was also seen by the Guatemalan military camp which we were observing. As they were unaware of its cause, panic ensued which enabled us to get a good idea of the full strength of their base.

Which just goes to prove "every cloud has a silver lining" . . . although, in this case, it may not have been silver!

Derek Joss

Lights on tights

On a Saturday night, at Farnborough, (the barracks of the 4th Royal Tank Regiment), there was always an entertainment put on by ENSA. But someone couldn't have been over-sensitive about the needs of the troops.

The entertainment for 1,000 rough soldiers was a second class ballet troupe with excerpts from *Swan Lake* and *Coppelia* and so on.

The troupe retired hurt at the interval after many indecent and raucous shouts from the troops like: "Look at the size of his whatsit!" and "Look at his b****ks!" The more reasonable of us were sorry for them, but they were no-hopers from the word go."

John Carmichael

The Search for Uncle Joe

Pte. 2716 Joseph Henry Curry, died on July 24, 1916, while serving with the 2nd Battalion, the Royal Warwickshire Regiment. Like many other families, research into the First World War and the part played by relatives became a near-obsession for Bob Curry. His search produced the most unexpected result.

On another trip to the Somme we bought (yet another) book about the battle. It carried a photograph of "some members of the 2nd Battalion, the Royal Warwickshire Regiment, enjoying a hot meal before battle."

I remembered this as an interesting fact, but not much more. On the return journey to Calais, however, we were half-watching a video on the coach of one of the BBC programmes on the Somme. It included some original battlefield film, including a sequence which ended up with the group shown in the picture in the book.

The photograph was accredited to the Imperial War Museum. Telephone calls to very helpful and supportive officials, resulted in us ordering the video set. In an attempt to create something and also to finish off the film in my camera, I attempted to take some stills from the television screen.

When I collected the film I flipped quickly through the prints. A face jumped out at me from one shot taken from the TV screen!

It looked like my father as a young man. I suspected that it might be a case of seeing what I wanted to see, so I kept quiet about it. I tried to look indifferent while I showed the photographs to my wife - and fellow WW1 addict - Marilyn. She picked out the same print and the same face!

After some fancy computer scanning of early photographs of my father, comparisons with all available relatives' likenesses were made. We had a match. We were convinced we had found Uncle Joe!

Reviewing the video yet again, and, this time knowing where to look, the likeness to my father was uncanny. Not only was there significant physical resemblance, but the body language, the way he stood, the way he moved, and way he turned his head, all made it seem as if we were watching my father.

We contacted our friends at the Imperial War Museum. As helpful as ever, they arranged an appointment at the Film Archive Department. Viewing their 35mm copy of the original film on an editing machine we could see the likeness with incredible clarity.

We were convinced. They added their expertise, reviewed our evidence, and *they* were convinced. We *had* found Uncle Joe!

We chose three specific and different frames which they arranged to have printed for just a few pounds.

So we now have a photograph of Joe and can see a face that nobody in the family has seen for more than 80 years. We now have a face to put to the man whose last journey we have been trying to reconstruct and we can see him as he was a couple of weeks before he died - a young man laughing with his comrades.

Bob Curry

Mystery passenger

On return from the Falklands I was the reporting officer on the aircraft, the link man between the RAF crew and the passengers, all of whom were relieved to be returning to the UK.

I was given the passenger manifest by the loadmaster and, taking my job seriously, I did a head count of the weary passengers. We were one short. I tried again but the numbers didn't add up. By this time we were airborne and nobody, but nobody, would want to return to the bleak windswept Falkland Islands to collect a passenger who had slipped through the check-in procedure.

I could pretend that the numbers were correct, but, sooner or later, the deficiency would be discovered. So I went around the aircraft checking off names against the manifest. The first was an Air Vice Marshal who was sitting beside me and wondered what all the fuss was about.

Cpl. Driver was the missing man. Blast Cpl. Driver! How could he have missed the flight when everybody was so anxious to leave? I duly reported it to the loadmaster who scanned the list impassively. He tapped the name of the missing Cpl. and shouted in my ear: "He *is* on board!"

"He's not!" I replied indignantly.

The loadmaster pointed vigorously to the freight compartment. "He's in a coffin travelling back to the UK."

Aubrey Chalmers

Wun flung dung

In the early days (*at Chung-Song POW Camp, North Korea*) one special outside concert which we were encouraged to put on for some Chinese festival or other was highly entertaining as it included a fast talking Cockney called Bill Sykes.

Bill departed from the script given by the Chinese censor and they could not understand his Cockney slang. For 20 minutes he kept the audience doubled up with laughter telling jokes about the Chinese.

He ended with the following:

They seek him here,
They seek him there,
They seek Old Mousy everywhere.
Will he be shot,
Or will he be hung,
That damned elusive Mousy Dung.

The English pronunciation of Mao Tse-tung is elusive enough, but, when uttered in Cockney, "Mousy Dung" was very difficult for Chinese political instructors and interpreters, who spoke fair English, to understand. The enthusiasm with which the verse was greeted aroused their suspicion and they called the speaker off the stage with the rest of the cast and asked them to explain.

They said they knew it was *supposed* to be funny - but not *that* funny. They did not understand it and they did not want it repeated. So they stopped the concert.

The Chinese brought in a travelling opera group to do a propaganda play one evening in the late summer of 1951. It was to be the first of a series but they totally failed at their first attempt.

"The White-haired Girl", as the play was known, was a highly acclaimed opera and the theme was the rape of a peasant girl by a rich landlord. The Chinese put everything they had into it. There was a large Army band with male and female singers. On stage there was full lighting and curtains, real furniture, a machine to make snow and another to produce thunder and lightning.

But the presentation was lost on all of us hungry POWs crowded, miserable and cold, on the parade ground for nearly six hours.

We applauded joyfully every time the girl got raped by the landlord and hissed at the wrong places, much to the disgust of the Chinese.

Henry O'Kane

'Splice the Mainbrace'

On May 7, 1945, *HMS Vanity* returned to Rosyth having, once again, completed another North Sea-East Coast convoy duty. We were fully expecting to have a short break before setting sail escorting another convoy down the East Coast, calling in at Immingham and then down to Sheerness.

Our Captain informed us that we would be "flashing up" and setting off at 5 am the very next morning. We were not too chuffed about this but, orders being orders, sure enough we were out of the pens, steaming under the Forth Bridge and out into the North Sea dead on time.

I closed up on my radar set (type 271 - five inch screen, hand-operated aerial) and, other than marker buoys, found no other ship let alone a convoy.

At 11 am on May 8, 1945 the Captain tannoyed "Splice the mainbrace. The war in Europe is over!"

We followed the instructions to a man! We were, however, not to return to Rosyth until early on May 9. *HMS Vanity* had been kept out at sea so that the ship's company could not indulge in the end of war celebrations taking place in Edinburgh on the night of May 8.

Apparently there were already enough rough sailors in the city that night!

Geoffrey Barwell

An arresting moment

After spending eighteen hair-raising months on airfield duty in Gibraltar, followed by some time in North Africa, then two further years in India, my war - along with several hundred others - was coming to an end.

We were all kicking our heels in Bombay, impatiently waiting for a ship home and, at last, peace. After a few hilarious weeks, being more than a little exuberant, I was called to report to the guard room and informed that Red Cap was waiting for me.

I was horrified! I racked my brains for my worst misdemeanour. Visions of not going home filled my head.

But there in the guard room, smart in his No 2s, stood my old school mate from my own village in the UK. We had a wonderful reunion and both returned to our village in 1946.

The sequel is that, a few years later, he was able to escort me again . . . as best man at my wedding. Then he helped to celebrate our Golden Anniversary.

It all goes to prove that some Red Caps can be human at times.

John S. Slade

Cell by date

After completing six weeks training at Budbrooke Barracks, Warwick, then a further two months in Scotland, I joined the 5th Battalion, Queen's Own Cameron Highlanders, 51st Division, as a driver. Then I embarked from Dover for Belgium and Ostend to join the Battalion in the winter of 1944.

Slowly we advanced through Belgium and Holland towards the Reichswald Forest in Germany, checking and clearing the ground as we progressed.

Suddenly a shell exploded! I felt pain in my leg. "Bloody Hell! My foot's gone!"

I went down and medics soon came to my aid. They checked my leg and remarked that it was still intact. But, as they tried to help me up blood was streaming from my arm. I tried to move it but failed.

"How can a damaged arm give you a pain in the leg?" asked the medic. Along with a number of my mates I was taken to a field hospital and, after a few days, flown to Brugge and the British 110 BLA hospital for further treatment. I went back to the UK on sick leave from Ostend.

After my return to duty I was transferred to the 2nd Battalion Gordon Highlanders for re-grouping to Tripoli. I was surprised to meet an old school pal William Makepeace. We returned to Brigadoon Barracks, Aberdeen, to be demobbed and, on arrival late at night, the only places available were in the cells at the guard room.

After a restless night the guard called to wake us. Thinking we were prisoners he shouted orders to dress and fall in for inspection. Thank God somebody came in time to explain!

Ronald Sheasby

Off the men you ...

One of the cooks (in Borneo) was a great practical joker and when you came in at night you would climb into bed and be greeted with a "French bed". You want to try getting into one of those after a skinfull. A "French bed" is one where the bottom sheet has been folded in half and made out to look like normal two sheets on a bed. But will only let you get half way down.

Another favourite trick of his was to put a snake in your bed which really freaked me out since I have a phobia about them.

He ended up being banned from the room and slept in a tent on the lawn outside the billet. His life would have been in jeopardy if he set foot in the room without an invitation. He stayed there for the next two years!

Ian Read

Tooth and nail

Things and incidents that happen to you during service in the Forces are always a source of discussion.

On joining the Air Force at the tender age of 18, going through the usual dental inspection, I was informed I had insufficient teeth to masticate (chew) properly. I would, therefore, have to have false teeth to make up the loss!

In due course I was kitted out with the teeth. On my next visit to the Mess I tried to master the art of eating with these newly-gained appliances. It was a total disaster. After a number of attempts to master the teeth I gave up and consigned them to a sock and placed them at the bottom of my kit.

The teeth travelled with me and, as they were on issue to me and had to be accounted for, were duly looked after at the bottom of my kit.

While serving in Burma we had been on corned beef and issue biscuits for many months and one day I had a very sore gum and discovered I had started to grow a wisdom tooth. I reported to the MO that I was having difficulty in eating as my false teeth would not lie due to the appearance of the new tooth.

He advised the nearest dentist was at the IGH (Indian General Hospital) in Chittagong and that I would have to make my own way there.

We had a plane going to North Assam to collect spares. So I had a lift for some 400 miles to a railhead and caught the train to Chittagong and reported to the IGH a week after leaving the squadron.

The dentist inspected the offending tooth, took the false teeth from me, and told me to report back in three months.

The return journey was made and, in due course, the repeat journey was accomplished to the IGH. The dentist took a look at the new tooth, gave me an injection, and pulled it out. He stated that the false teeth would now fit.

All in all they did me good service. I had almost a month out of the jungle and had a change of food at the IGH.

Cyril Reynolds

Snakes alive!

We were in an outpost at Tebadu, Borneo, about half a mile from the Indonesian border.

Stand-to was only for half an hour's duration, but the first few seconds seemed like hours. Time was irrelevant there, the days were long and the nights even longer. Guard duty was a nightly affair and we stood and patrolled the gun emplacement for an hour on our own.

One night when I was on guard I had to look out for a Gurkha patrol coming in and I also had to listen out for their call sign on the radio to let me know they were approaching the clearing.

I went into the command post where the radio was situated. The CP was lit only by a torch bulb which gave a dim light just above the radio. All of a sudden I heard rustling by my side. I froze. I knew that everyone else was in bed and asleep. I snapped on my torch quickly and, in the beam, there was the biggest snake I had ever seen. It was ginormous!

The snake was looking at me and I was looking at him. Suddenly we both darted for the door at the same time. I think the snake won by a short head. Needless to say, I didn't follow to see where it went. I was too frightened even to note what variety it was.

At the end of my shift I had still heard nothing from the Gurkha patrol. So I went to their quarters. I found that they had returned without being seen and thought they would make me sweat a little for a joke. Having sweated already in the CP I managed to laugh with them, relieved that they all got back in one piece.

The same could not be said for some of their prisoners who were minus a head or a limb. That particular Gurkha unit certainly lived up to their reputation as fearsome fighters and I was glad that we were on the same side.

Ian Read

Jungle fighter Ian Read. He survived an ambush but ended up with a lasting horror of snakes.

The Spanish succession

I arrived in this country at the age of 12. I was one of the 4,000 children evacuated from the north of Spain during the civil war of 1937.

I came by sea to Southampton and years later, at the age of 16, I was sent to work in a munitions factory in Coventry. As all of us know this industrial city went through hell during the war. I was there when the late King George V1 and the Queen Mother visited the city after the worst blitz.

At 19 I decided to volunteer and joined the Royal Navy. Little did I know that a few years later, some ten days after 'D' Day, I would find myself, with others, helping His Majesty the King, plus all the top brass that followed, to come aboard HM Motor Launch 147.

The sea was very choppy when we had to moor by the gangway of *HMS Arethusa,* the ship in which the King travelled from England to Normandy. It was decided to tie up alongside the ship after the chippies had made a makeshift ladder. This hung over the side enabling the visitors to board our boat. We took her as close as we could to the beach where they boarded a waiting DUKW *(a six-wheeled amphibious truck known as a "duck" and capable of carrying 25 troops)* and finally landed on the beach where General Montgomery and his troops were waiting.

After nearly five months non-stop active service in Normandy we were summoned to Pompey (Portsmouth) where we were ordered to escort a convoy of landing craft for the landing at Walchern Island off the Dutch coast. Our CO, Lieut. Commander A.S. Bennett was senior officer of the flotilla.

I relieved the coxswain at the wheel. It was well after midnight when a landing craft accidentally hit us amidships during one of our manoeuvres. As a result, we were put out of action and it meant the end of Motor Launch 147.

I thought I was the only Spaniard to have served in the Royal Navy. But I was wrong.

When the Spanish monarchy was expelled and went into exile in 1931 (after the Revolution) there was a Prince serving in the Spanish Navy. He was Don Juan de Borbon, the father of the present King of Spain.

Because he had to leave his country the British Monarchy invited him to finish his naval career in the Royal Navy and this he did from 1931- 1936. In November 1987 the Admiralty granted him the role of "Honorary Admiral" for his service.

So, as you can see, I was the second Spaniard to have served in the Royal Navy during its history, albeit a "commoner".

After the war this Coventry kid applied for, and was granted, British Nationality in 1954. I am proud to have served in the Royal Navy and more so in the Coastal Forces.

Alfredo Ruiz

Southern discomfort

The Italians did not bother us much (*at an Italian POW camp at Chiavari, near Genoa*). Twice a day we had to line up to be counted. Not the simple operation one might imagine. We did our best to mess them about so that they could never get it right, which provided some light entertainment.

The camp commandant had the bright idea of giving us some work to keep us occupied. This involved us linking up in twos, each pair carrying a shallow metal bucket between them and being escorted through the gate to a dried up river bed which was situated between the camp and the road about 100 yards away.

At a given point each pair had to fill their bucket with stones and be escorted back to the camp where the stones were tipped into a heap. Having spent an hour or so repeating the operation we were dismissed, and another group loaded their buckets from the heap in the camp and took them back to the river bed and tipped them out.

This did not go on for long. Neither side was too enthusiastic about the idea and it did not provide a lot of job satisfaction.

Fred Frost

'Wormspeak'

The HQ British Forces Middle East was based in an office block in the centre of Riyadh, Saudi Arabia, during the Gulf War. All the road signs were, of course, in Arabic and christened "wormspeak" by the troops.

The route between the HQ in the city and the King Khalid International Airport (KKIA) was familiar and comparatively easy.

Sometimes, however, it was necessary to go to the British Embassy for a "conference", the only place in Saudi Arabia where it was possible to obtain a welcome gin and tonic. The problem was, however, that it was easy to get lost on the huge motorway system.

It was impossible to read the road signs - except for the one internationally recognised logo and sign for the airport.

On more than one occasion a bewildered driver was glad to follow the signs to the airport, travelling many miles out of town, to pick up the familiar route back to the British HQ.

Very few, apart from General Sir Peter de la Billiere, could speak Arabic.

Nevertheless, in this immense desert, where water was priced at about 25p per litre and petrol a mere 8p, I did come across an admirable effort in the use of English by an Arab trader. He put out a sign: "Bear wit out all ko hole."

Aubrey Chalmers

What a small world

An incident during the Burma War illustrates what a small world we live in . . .

After the retaking of Akyab Island, off the coast of Burma, I had to fly to Calcutta for spares.

On landing at Dum-Dum airstrip I was walking to the control tower to book in when a Flt. Lieutenant pilot stopped me and asked if I was from 194 Squadron. I confirmed I was. He asked for a lift back to the Squadron as he had been posted to us as a replacement pilot.

We had a few words of conversation and he said, "My cousin is with 194 Squadron."

I inquired who the cousin was.

"Cyril Reynolds."

"Hullo Cousin!" I replied.

We had not seen each other since we were about six years old. Our mothers were sisters.

He was posted again after about four months with our Squadron and we have not seen each other again since that time.

Cyril Reynolds

A riotous birthday

It was in a transit camp, in the middle of the desert in Egypt, that I celebrated my 21st birthday in a rather unconventional fashion.

In the afternoon two of us pooled our resources, following our week's leave (in Cairo), and managed to muster enough piastres for four cups of NAAFI tea each. At 6 pm I had to report to the Regimental Office to receive my orders for duty as Camp Police.

A bombardier and myself were given CP armbands and detailed to patrol the camp until midnight. My mate had done this before and knew the ropes. Consequently, we took up our position in the open air cinema, just a collection of chairs and tables bounded by an 8ft wooden wall.

Things went well as we watched the film, until the projector broke down. This did not please the audience of British, Australian, New Zealand and South African troops. In fact, when it broke down for the second and third time, they began throwing things at the screen and at each other.

The situation was rapidly getting rough. I turned to my fellow CP and asked: "What do we do now?"

He replied: "Put those armbands in our pockets and get out quick."

We spent the rest of my 21st birthday patrolling the area of camp as far away from the cinema as possible

Fred Frost

Sparks sent flying

In Italy Harry and I were detailed to look after the supply of electricity to the quarters of the "heavy brass" which were situated within the grounds of the Palace in Caserta, *(Caserta, about 20 miles north of Naples, was the Allied HQ in Italy.)*

From our time in North Africa we had learned how to give each other an alternate day off. It was Harry's day on.

We both suspected that someone was using an electric fire because the diesel generator which supplied the General's Mess, 250 yards away, was playing up. The system was overloaded. Had it been supplying lighting alone there would have been no problem. Harry was only half aware that the task he had set himself was nigh impossible as he examined the machine. A voice asked: "What's the trouble?"

Without raising his head a very angry Harry replied: "The f*** trouble is that you can't get a f*** pint out of a f*** half-pint pot."

At that stage Harry looked up to see the speaker and a young aide was poised to take Harry's name and number. At that moment Harry thought he had bought his lot - but the voice said: "Leave it!"

Some time later, on the last Friday of April 1945, I doubt if Harry would have taken his day off in Naples had we known that a million troops were about to surrender to Field Marshal Alexander.

He went off and I said I could handle any problems. I ambled along a well-trodden path through the Palace grounds towards the two newly-installed generators.

I started up No 1 generator. The two meters showed an upwards move on the dials . . . then fell back. I started generator No 2. The meters stayed at zero.

In times of crisis it seems that other forces take over. My thoughts were sorted out under the shower and the dripping water made me realise what the problem was. It was probably water getting into the lamp holders surrounding a nearby compound which had been recently erected.

It was not occupied by POWs then, though we saw it being erected in quick time. A lot was happening, there were some very high ranking people around, and something big was on. But we were kept in the dark.

With purposeful stride I went to the sentry at the compound gate. God was on my side. The sentry recognised me and issued an instruction which I can now translate as "Go away Sparky!"

I heard myself saying: "Turn out the guard! I'm coming in."

I explained first what I thought to be the problem to an American orderly officer and how it was necessary to improvise a remedy. Then I was interviewed by two RE officers and the tape and the ladder I needed were found. I started to tape up each lamp holder to make it waterproof, not the sort of thing you could do now a days.

As I checked each lamp holder I was amused to see the embarrassment of the "heavy brass" as a high-ranking German officer questioned the presence of the ladder and myself. He seemed very surprised to see me there. I never discovered who he was, but I realised later that he was there to negotiate the armistice.

They eased him out of view. Your senses tell you that I had stumbled on something rather important.

Shortly after that we went on leave to Sorrento and Amalfi. We even visited a nunnery which was interesting. The coast was lovely and we were determined to see as much of Italy as we could and it was all rather wonderful. I must admit going AWOL at this time though we were never disciplined for it.

We went to Amalfi and that very night news came from the Italian population that the war in Europe was over. An Italian told us and we couldn't believe it for a long time. The Italians bought us drinks. Lots of drinks. The next morning we woke up in a strange hotel, the Italians having put us to bed.

Harry went through his pockets and commented: "The war *must* be over. I have all my money and I've spent nothing!"

Ernest Garwood

It was not surprising that Ernest Garwood caused some alarm and embarrassment for senior Allied officers because he had stumbled on top secret negotiations with German Generals about the German surrender in Italy. To begin with nobody at Caserta, except Field Marshal Alexander, his C in C, and the Chief Signals Officer, new anything about it.

After many secret and informal meetings in Switzerland, starting in November 1944, Field Marshal Alexander sent two Generals, one American and one British from Caserta, to meet the Germans in Switzerland in March 1945. It was agreed that emissaries could visit Caserta. Despite Hitler's orders that the German Army in Italy had to stand fast, four senior German officers were flown in secret to Caserta where, no doubt, they could not understand why a soldier from the Royal Signals was perched on a ladder looking over the hastily erected compound in which the secret talks were taking place.

On April 29, 1945, the surrender of German forces on the Italian front was signed..

It became effective on Wednesday May 2. Six days later, while Ernest Garwood and his fellow Signaller were enjoying themselves in Amalfi, the war in Europe ended. It is generally considered that the surrender in Italy shortened the war by several weeks since the German Army, to the north, was placed in an impossible military situation after the surrender of units in Italy.

Benediction

One of the many little girls evacuated from London was going to bed on her first evening in the country.

"Did you say your prayers before going to bed darling?" her hostess asked.

The little girl said she did.

"Well then, kneel down and I'll listen as your Mummy does."

The kiddie repeated as usual "Now I lay me down to sleep", and then improvised a postscript of her own.

"And God, please protect Daddy and Mummy from those German bombs. And do, dear God, take good care of yourself - because if anything happens to you, we're sunk."

From the "Canterbury Tales News Sheet", HM Troopship *Canterbury* . The newsletter was displayed on our troopship on April 20, 1941 as we sailed from Durban to Port Said.

Fred Frost

Chapter 5

Let the Rest of the World go by

The pilot fell for the girl in the control tower

In love's wars, he who flieth is conqueror.
T. FULLER, PROVERBS 1732.

Snuggle and Embrace

In January 1939 I was 18 years old and in August of that year I was at a Territorial Army camp at Bridlington with the 121st Field Regiment, Royal Artillery. We went for a fortnight - but they kept us for six years!

After some training in Leeds where we were stationed, all 18 year olds were transferred to a heavy anti aircraft battery on the South Coast. We were equipped with 3.7 ack-ack guns with which we did out best to defend Plymouth.

Then, on daily Orders appeared a notice asking for volunteers for aircrew duties. Having always wanted to fly Spitfires I volunteered straight away, took the usual academic and fitness tests, and went on to train as a pilot in England and Canada where I got my wings.

After various postings six of us came together as a crew at an operational training unit in Scotland from where we were posted to 295 Squadron, 38 Group RAF, a special duties squadron based at RAF Harwell in Oxfordshire and frequently at RAF Rivenhall in Essex.

Our operational duties included towing gliders - for D Day, Arnhem and the airborne crossings of the Rhine - dropping supplies to the Resistance fighters in France, the Netherlands and Norway, and to the airborne forces fighting for the bridge at Arnhem and also dropping paratroops.

We flew Albemarles initially and converted to Stirlings in time for Operation "Market Garden", the valiant attempt by the airborne forces to capture the bridge over the Rhine at Arnhem.

It was while we were at RAF Rivenhall that I was fortunate enough to meet Margaret who became my ever loving wife. She was a WAAF who had been on plotting duties with 9 Group RAF and had moved to Flying Control duties with 38 Group RAF.

I was in charge of night flying one night in October 1944 and, on going up into Flying Control, there was this gorgeous WAAF. A real cracker!

The Flying Control call sign happened to be "Snuggle" and our Squadron call sign was "Embrace"

I was the lucky one and Snuggle and I married in September 1946 and we are still happily together after 55 years.

Sqn Leader Roy Scott

I had to salute him!

I was a member of the Women's Auxiliary Air Force, the WAAF, during the 1939-45 War. After initial training at Morecambe I was posted to Preston which was the headquarters of No. 9 Group. My job was on the secret list and we were called "Clerks Special Duties". Actually, our job was to plot the movement of all aircraft, our own and those of the enemy, using long poles to move markers on a table map. From Preston I went to Netheravon, Wiltshire, where the glider pilots were trained. I worked in the Operations Room and later at Marks Hall in Essex. The Americans had just moved out and left lots of lovely food behind!

It was here that we heard our first "buzz bombs" and "doodle bugs" which were very frightening as, when they cut out, no one knew where they were going to drop.

Towards the end of the war, when the enemy was infiltrating less and less, I was transferred to the control tower on an airfield called Rivenhall in Essex. It was here that I met Flt. Lieutenant (Later Squadron Leader) Roy Scott where he was in charge of night flying.

We were not supposed to go out with Officers but, of course, we did. Whenever we went to a camp dance the band always played *Let the Rest of the World Go by* which remains our tune to this day.

You can imagine what it was like watching him take off and waiting . . . waiting and praying for his safe return.

Runway romance. Roy Scott, the bomber pilot on SOE missions, who fell in love with the girl in the control tower.

Margaret Scott, the WAAF who waited with her heart in her mouth for the safe return of her boyfriend. He would sing to her over the aircraft radio.

He flew a huge Stirling aircraft which either towed a glider (he took part in D Day, the Rhine Crossing and Arnhem) or dropped spies or supplies to the Resistance.

When I saw him walking through the camp I had to salute him!

On Valentines Day he sent me a bouquet which contained 105 roses which I shared with all the girls who lived in the same hut as myself. Once he sang *I once had a heart Margarita* over the radio which was against all the rules.

Each year we attend services in remembrance of the actions he undertook and, although we are all now Golden Oldies, we have many treasured memories which we share with our friends in the RAF and Glider Pilot Regiment.

I simply had to tell you about our meeting which took place so long ago and is just as important to us now as it was then. On September 14, 2001, Roy and I celebrated 55 years marriage - the Emerald Anniversary.

Margaret E.M. Scott, (Cpl. Margaret Sharrott)

Chapter 6

Many a Lucky Escape

This is the Army Mr Jones
IRVING BERLIN, 1942.

The Fareham rope trick

The place: A Barrage Balloon Station, Fareham, Hants., in 1943.

I was a WAAF operator assigned to one of the balloon guy ropes which ran through "spiders" fixed to the ground. Each rope was released separately on a word of command by the duty sergeant to the winch driver.

One day my rope was released by the winch driver without the correct command!

I was hauled up about 30 feet into the air. I slid down rapidly, my hands burning on the rope and I landed flat on my back . . . very hard!

Fortunately our station was directly opposite the land-based *HMS Collingwood* and the Royal Navy Ambulance very quickly took me to Netley Hospital where I spent a month lying on boards and having my hands treated for rope burns.

I never returned to Barrage Balloons. In fact, shortly after this, as enemy air attacks increased in the Southampton area, the balloons were manned by RAF male personnel.

Even now, sixty years on, the palms of my hands are still bright red!

Elsie Rushall

Surprise levitation. Elsie Rushall, the WAAF forgot to let go of barrage balloon cable.

44

Flying bomb

We were sailing on *HMS Orion* between Sicily and Italy, through the Straits, when the radar picked up an aircraft high up and slightly astern. Then a smaller craft separated from it and gradually lost height until it was positioned immediately above us. It was identified as a flying bomb!

No matter what evasive action the ship took the bomb, controlled from the aircraft above, followed us.

Suddenly, it dived absolutely vertically, missing us by a few feet astern. The explosion which followed was like a dozen depth charges going off at once. It lifted the stern of the ship and carried us forward on the crest of a wave.

After the war, I was reading about the doodlebug attacks on the South of England and it mentioned that one had been launched from an aircraft against a ship in the Straits of Sicily - and the attack failed.

A miss is as good as a mile, especially at sea.

John Curtis

HMS Orion *was a 1932 cruiser of 7,270 tons. She was built by Vicars Armstrong and was sold for scrap in 1949 after a distinguished World War II record.*

How we survived the Barn Massacre

While the evacuation of 350,000 troops went ahead at Dunkirk, men of the battle weary 2nd. Battalion, the Royal Warwickshire Regiment, helped to provide a rearguard action to hold up the advancing German forces. Eventually they were overrun, out of ammunition, and captured by the SS Lieberstandarte Adolf Hitler Division which took no prisoners. On May 28, 1940 the British troops were marched to a barn at Wormhout and massacred. Bert Evans, who was 19 at the time, was one survivor. Alfred Tombs, aged 28, was another.

We took up our position during the afternoon of May 27. There had been much air activity all day and we could see the smoke columns from Dunkirk. We spent the night of May 27-28 waiting for a dawn attack. The attack came at 0745 and refugees were streaming down the road from Esquelbecq to Wormhout. Vehicles came down the road and they were knocked out. The Germans renewed their attack about noon and it was supported by tanks. We took many casualties. There were just too many tanks to be halted.

It appears that the German commander General Dietrich was impatient at the progress and, with a driver, set off along the road to Wormhout. His vehicle was hit and burst into flames. The driver was killed and the General just had time to take cover in a ditch.

We began to withdraw to the houses. Many were captured and rounded up and some were shot on the spot. About 50 of us, including some Gunners and soldiers from the Cheshire Regiment, were rounded up and marched to a farm where, apparently a senior SS officer berated the NCO of the escort for taking prisoners.

Now we were marched across sodden fields and the going was heavy. One man who could not keep up was shot. We reached a small field and at the entrance was a small roughly constructed building with a thatched roof. It would be about 21 ft. by 10ft. 6 ins. This cowshed was open at one end with a door in the left hand wall, almost blocked by hardened cow droppings.

Parallel to the end wall was a row of trees and, about 70 yards away from the shed, at the end of the line of trees, was a stagnant pond.

Everyone was pushed into the shed. I stood at the entrance with Captain James Lynn-Allen. Captain Lynn-Allen remonstrated with one of the SS guards who spoke English. He said that there were wounded in the group and that there was no room for the men to lie down. The German said that where they were going there would be room enough. With that, he pulled a grenade from his boot and hurled it into the group. I felt a blow to my arm and I knew I had been badly wounded.

Capt. Lynn-Allen held my good arm and urged me to run. While the Germans sheltered from the explosions we dodged out of the side door and along the line of trees.

We got into the pond and tried to hide there. One of the guards saw us and shot Captain Lynn-Allen in the head. He fired three shots at me, one of which ricoched off a tree and hit me in the neck. I sank below the water and the guard left, thinking he had finished us off.

Bert Evans, survived the Wormhout Massacre by hiding in a pond.

46

I was able to leave the pond and hide. Later I made my way to the farmhouse and the farmer's daughter, who was about 11, tended my wounds and saved my life. I was captured at the farm and my shattered arm was later amputated.

The barn was demolished years ago but I keep returning to the spot. It is very emotional and I always cry. I keep returning because it keeps the memory alive. The whole thing is so impressed on my mind that I cannot ever forget the horror of it.

Bert Evans

As we were herded through a gate a tall thin SS officer kicked me in the backside. I'll never forget him. It was the man in charge, Wilhelm Mohnke. We were all pushed into a barn and one of our our officers complained about the way we were treated. I think they shot him.

Then the guards called for five to go outside. Nobody would move. Then one went and four followed him. They took them out into the field. I looked through a crack in the planking and I saw the first five being lined up and shot in the back. Another five were taken out and I heard more shots.

I was still inside the barn. Then I saw one of the SS guards bend down and take a stick grenade from his boot. He swung it in. I threw myself flat on the ground. I could smell the cordite as it exploded and I tried to bury my mouth below ground thinking there was gas. Two bodies landed on top of me.

A man in front of me was screaming that his leg had been damaged. He was close to my head. I heard one lad shout: "Shoot me, you bastards! shoot me!" They put one through his head between his eyes. Later he was still sitting upright with a hole in his head.

They went around shooting and eventually they left us thinking everyone was dead. I really thought I was going to die. They wanted no witnesses. I survived only because bodies were on top of me. I received shrapnel wounds in the leg and I was bleeding badly.

A small group of us crawled out of the barn and to a ditch where we crawled on our hands and knees to a farmhouse. I was afraid they might return and kill anyone who was alive. Eventually, with five others, I was captured while we were sheltering behind a hedge.

I was still afraid they were going to kill us. A German officer came over and said in perfect English: "It's all right. The war is over. You'll be in Berlin and we'll be in London."

We still thought we were going to die. One of our men pleaded on his knees not to be shot. The German officer said: "You've suffered enough" and his men gave us biscuits.

Alfred Tombs

Alf Tombs survived the massacre because he lay under a pile of bodies.

After initial attempts to take groups of prisoners before a firing squad the SS troops tried to speed up the massacre and fired at anyone standing, sitting or lying. The killers left about 19 wounded who did what they could for one another. The survivors were found later by regular German Army soldiers and were well treated and received hospital treatment. Nobody knows exactly how many were massacred. German troops buried the victims of the SS atrocity in the field. 36 bodies were later discovered and reburied in a local cemetery. Others, including the body of Capt. Lynn-Allen still lie in the field which, in November 2000 was acquired by the local residents to preserve it. Mohnke, later became a major general and was commander of Hitler's bunker. The perpetrators of the murder were never brought to justice.

'Condemned' men's last smoke

The Chinese called a halt near a dry gully that came down the side of a gently sloping hill. They then ordered us prisoners to spread ourselves along its length and then, for the first time, I saw the line of prisoners recently captured. There appeared to be about 40 in all, mostly RURs (Royal Ulster Rifles).

No sooner had we rested our tired bodies along the side of the gully than the Chinese soldiers came along and relieved us of any kit or equipment we had been carrying, searching each man, taking such items as fountain pens and watches.

Then occurred one of the most dramatic moments of captivity.

Some pessimistic character observed: "It is an ideal place for an execution!" And, in reality, it was.

However, everyone appeared to be very calm. No-one appeared to do anything.

We just sat around looking dumbfounded. It was all a bit of an anti-climax. We were all aware of, and some of us had witnessed, the many atrocities committed by the Communists up and down Korea.

As I sat there I did not feel assured by the safe conduct pass that had been given to me earlier in the day.

I had run out of cigarettes long before capture, but, on request, Tommy produced a crumpled packet of Philip Morris, the last remnants of an American 24-hour C ration pack. It contained seventeen rather battered and bruised specimens.

As condemned men, which was exactly how we felt, we would not have a last meal but we had our seventeen Philip Morris. These we divided up equally, eight and a half each, and promptly lit up with the intention of smoking our last smoke.

The morning had started foggy, thus we received no air cover, but, as we huddled in the gully with our cigarettes, I noticed then the blue of the sky and the brown scrub covered hills around us. There we sat smoking, remembering, and reminiscing about the good times at Brigade HQ and in Japan.

No sooner had we finished smoking the last of our cigarettes, which we were to regret later, than the Chinese hustled and herded us on.

We were rather relieved.

Henry O'Kane

Home on a wing and a prayer

I have a strong aversion to the use of the words "luck" or "fate".

A person should be in control of his own destiny. But what decides that destiny? Being in the wrong place at the wrong time? When my name was called by the Flight Commander and I was ordered to find my pilot, my family's good record of survival was to continue. Other men I knew were allocated the same chance and they did not survive.

I was 19. I pictured the pilot as a mature man in his late twenties. He was to be the captain of a four-engine bomber (Lancaster). When I first saw him I was not filled with confidence. He looked no older than 21 years and was a Canadian from Toronto!

The posting to an operational squadron was to 5 Group, 106 Squadron at Syerston, some 14 miles from Nottingham. The Wing Commander was Gibson, of Dambusters fame. The operational tour was 30 and the survival rate was low. My first trip was on November 20, 1942, to Turin and my last was on April 4, 1943 to Kiel. I was allowed to complete my tour with 28 trips as I had missed one operation while I was ill with flu.

Survival was a mixture of crew efficiency and luck or good fortune, with a dash of my family's survival record.

On trip 7, returning from Essen, the photo flash, which was carried in an open chute beneath the mid upper turret, and should have been dropped with the bombs, exploded inside the aircraft. There was a large hole beneath the turret. When we examined the damage and realised how close the rudder controls were to the explosion, good fortune had smiled upon us.

On one trip, on the routine route to Berlin and while approaching Denmark, changing course was imprecise. We had altered course when, out of the darkness from port, came a Halifax. He had not altered course. Near-collisions today are reported if they are within 500 feet but to say the Halifax was 20 feet over the top of us would not be an exaggeration!

Mid-air collisions were an ever present danger. We avoided the Halifax by pure chance. At night, of course, there was no visual avoidance.

When I finished my first tour on April 4, 1943, I was an old head and would be celebrating my 20th birthday in June. On completion of my second tour I was just two months past my 21st birthday.

For my second tour I was posted to the Pathfinders 637 Squadron, 8 Group, stationed at Downham Market, a short distance from Kings Lynn.

The targets were a lot easier. A tour was completed on a count of points. I cannot remember the exact point count. Germany was still the most difficult and, if I remember correctly, we got two points for one light operation, and these I show in my log in green ink.

All the duties were designed to mark the target with coloured bombs. As the raid progressed we had to keep the target marked and keep it centred to avoid bombing short of the target area.

First on target were the illuminators followed by the primary visual marker. Then the Master Bomber came next and assessed where the markers were in relation to the aiming point. The Master Bomber remained on target until the raid was complete, broadcasting to the main force where to direct their bombs. It was a hazardous duty since you were always well below the main force, crossing the target area more than once, and circling the area all the time. I did five Master Bombers trips though it will be appreciated that the pilot was MB.

I left the crew at the end of my 36th trip. "Come on John, let's do a hundred trips!" Good sense prevailed. Whatever the reason it was yet another decision for my survival.

On the next trip my replacement was wounded in the head by shrapnel. He was much *shorter* than I was and he received a scalp wound. I was four inches *higher* and where it would have hit, had I been there, I can only surmise. Perhaps they did complete their 100 trips.

John Hadlon

John Hadlon was a rear gunner on a four-engine Lancaster, a bomber which had a crew of seven and a range of 2,530 miles. It was armed with six .303 machine guns and the bomb load was 22,000 lbs. Bomber

Command suffered such heavy losses in the latter part of 1943 that raids on German cities, including Hamburg and Berlin, were discontinued in favour of coastal targets like Kiel. During 20,000 sorties on Berlin, commencing in November 1943, 1,047 aircraft were lost and another 1,682 damaged. More than 14,650 of the sorties were flown by Lancasters which were considered to be the best of the heavy bombers even though the aircraft had light armament.

Altogether 55,000 Bomber Command personnel were killed during the war and it is estimated that crews had a one in 20 chance of not surviving a mission. They had to fly 30 missions before their tour finished.

Flare for trouble

On the return from a bombing raid over Germany our Lancaster was one of six planes fitted with a "Million Candlepower" flare, carried in a flare chute. The flare was to be ejected after "bombs gone" message. This flare lit up the area of the attack to photograph automatically the success (or otherwise) of the mission.

On this night the wireless operator, whose responsibility it was to check the chute before returning to base, discovered that the flare had jammed in the chute.

The pilot hastily ordered the crew members to attempt to free the flare. Meanwhile I sat trapped in my navigator's cubbyhole anxiously listening to the crew crashing and banging away at the offending flare. I expected that at any minute we would all be blown out of the sky.

Fortunately the lads hacked it away and, once more, we returned safely home.

Bernard W. Rushall

Bernard Rushall, a flare stuck in a chute threatened to engulf his Lancaster bomber.

Emergency exit

In the autumn of 1943 we were part of the first convoy to go through the Mediterranean, bound for Egypt, following the fall of France in 1940.

In the event of an attack the drill was that all troops should sit at their mess tables until they were given orders to climb the gangway in the holds. Officers and NCOs were stationed to control any evacuation in an orderly manner.

South of Crete we were subjected to bombing and torpedo attacks, some of the missiles being aerial torpedoes.

Suddenly there was a loud explosion and the ship shuddered but continued safely on its way. All eyes had been turned to us at the exits to see if the troops were to be allowed to move!

The bomb had penetrated the decks and left the ship through a port hole, *exploding outside.* Unfortunately, on the way, it killed one man who was sitting in his mess deck. We had been very lucky.

Dr. Ronald Bower

My greatest role

Alastair Bannerman was a professional actor. But, as a soldier, he played the greatest role of his career. He was captured by the fanatical 21st Panzer Division while serving with the Royal Warwickshire Regiment in the fierce battles which followed the Normandy landings in June 1944. He saved his life - by acting dead and pretending to be a corpse.

Suddenly an 88 got our range and sent up our Bren Gun Carrier in a deafening explosion, with all our ammunition, knocking us sideways. The next few minutes, I felt, were my last. Hunted, and flat on my belly, I could hear my heart pounding into the earth.

The wheat was only too revealing as we crushed it flat, and soon I could hear shouts approaching and the noise of tank tracks.

I only had a grenade, so I pulled out the pin, having a vague idea of still defending myself. I peered up over the wheat and, to my despair and horror, saw a German pointing a Schmeizer at me and shouting and jerking his gun to tell me to get up.

I saw just behind him three of my chaps with their hands up and a tracked vehicle covering us all. I still held the pinless grenade and tried vainly to wedge it in the hard earth. But the handle started to spring away and I had to grab it again.

So I stood up with the grenade in my right hand and my arms above my head. I couldn't throw it as I should have killed my own men, besides a certain death myself, so I pointed to it with my left hand and said "grenade" rather feebly. The German bellowed again, so I chucked it hard over my shoulder behind me and it went off a few yards away in the wheat. I was then marched off with my men.

Why I didn't get shot outright I shall never know.

As we were marched into the wood my Corporal said: "This is it, sir, I'm afraid."

I must say I felt we were going to be lined up and shot, but I contrived to say: "Nonsense, we shall be all right."

After this tension of dark bushes we emerged into a clearing where various Germans lounged about.

Although it was still a shock to feel we were captured, the thing which no one ever entertains or imagines, I could still notice the cool nonchalance of these troops. Tall and blonde, with long peak caps, they seemed vastly amused by the sight of us in our camouflaged steel helmets and all our khaki palaver. Remarkably efficient and cool they looked, and I was not surprised to find they were the 21st Panzer Division.

We were told to sit down under a tree, and I hoped my Captain's pips would remain unnoticed. It gave me a chance to warn the men what to say and what not to say and generally keep our little group together. But, when the questioning came, the man concerned became so abusive and threatening that I felt I should try and effect a little rank-consciousness in him, and insisted as an English "hauptmann" on seeing an officer. I was then separated from my men and we sat and waited. Some Germans had caught a cow, with great shouts of laughter, and we were offered some warm milk direct from the udder which we gratefully accepted. These Germans were quite friendly, unlike the rabid interrogator.

Suddenly, a German Jeep-type car drove up and an officer stepped out with the interrogator. Young and handsome, he came over to me and told me in English to accompany him. I asked where to, but he refused to answer. Somehow I felt loath to leave my old comrades and even this spot seemed more friendly than the unknown.

The officer got in behind me with a revolver in his hand and we drove off. I confess I did not like it.

As we came out of the wood into the village street there was a sudden burst of firing up the road the way I had come originally, and excited shouts from the Germans.

The driver of our car lost his head, failed to take the corner and drove into the far wall of the street. I stood up, wondering what to do, and happened to glance around. The whole street was in uproar, the driver had jumped out and the officer as well. The latter was standing behind me, and, as I turned, he was pointing his revolver at me.

I knew with certainty that he was going to shoot me. I suppose he could have done little else if an attack was developing. As he fired, some sixth sense or providence made me fall in a limp heap over the windscreen. I never saw him again. I suppose he thought he had shot me, and had no time to find out.

I lay there acting the part of a corpse as I never acted before. I didn't dare move. I let my arms swing limp and my neck, and as I hung, I prayed.

I could hear the engine of the car still ticking over. The noise echoes in my subconscious mind to this day, together with a bedlam of crashes, and the high hum of bullets as the street round me seemed to fill with a fury of sound, signifying extinction.

I lay there, waiting while the noise beat on, waiting while tracks passed me, waiting for the sound of a British voice. At last I thought I heard one. I moved slowly, cautiously, and then - a hard barrel jabbed into my back and a furious guttural German voice shouted at me. I turned and saw a black-bearded scruffy German with a particularly villainous face wearing a new type of black SS uniform.

However my luck held and once again I was marched into the wood and my men grinned at me and called out: "Didn't expect to see you again sir!"

"I'm damned lucky to be here," I grinned back.

On the way I had passed a number of fresh corpses on the road, one an officer I recognised. Some new attack had failed. What was happening? What had happened to the Battalion?

I sat down again under the trees while the Germans wandered casually around. They gave us a mug of wine to drink which was delicious, probably some miraculous vintage which they had looted from a cellar. Suddenly, everyone tensed and crouched as the sound of an express train approached, tore over our heads with a monstrous clap, and exploded in the wheatfield.

*'My greatest theatrical role.'
By acting the part of a dead
man Alastair Bannerman
saved his life.*

54

At last, the Germans showed a little concern and donned steel helmets. We were given long-handled shovels and told to dig - which we did enthusiastically. I realised that at last it was the Naval fire support from the *Warspite's* 16-inch guns ranging on this wood. Fortunately the trains continued to hurtle over us into the wheat field with great cracks like a giant ring-master's whip.

We were all - Germans and English alike - now in slit trenches and I found myself sharing one with a German lance-corporal. We started chatting and he said we should soon be back in the sea. I agreed that the war would soon be over, but that it was we who would decide it, and the fact that we had landed was the proof of our future victory. He roared with laughter about our tanks, and said a lot I couldn't understand.

He insisted on showing me photos of his girl friend in Hamburg, and I, politely, returned the gesture by showing my wife and children. The whole irony of the situation seemed quite extraordinary. War seemed so unnecessary when ordinary men of each side could still be human and friendly. I hadn't met any Nazis then.

The noise increased again with the addition of small arms fire and not so far

Alastair Bannerman's own drawing of how he shared a trench with his captor while under a British attack. They exchanged family photographs.

away. I heard later it was the Norfolks counter-attacking to help out my Battalion which had been shot to pieces on the far edge of this large wood.

I wondered what I should do if, suddenly, I saw our own uniforms rushing these positions. It would have been very tricky and we should probably have been shot by one side or the other.

Alastair Bannerman

Mine Sweeping - the alternative way

Within hours of the end of the war in Europe and the surrender of German forces on May 8, 1945, HMS Vanity *was despatched with essential supplies for troops in Norway.*

We were ordered to take aboard and stow in the engine room as many large cardboard boxes as possible. These, we very soon discovered, contained smaller tin boxes of "iron rations" or "hard tack", a couple of very thick very hard ship's biscuits plus some very hard chocolate.

Needless to say we were not very interested in our cargo or the contents.
We were to "flash up" and deliver our cargo to the paratroops and service personnel in Norway. Immediately!

What a nightmare. When not closed up on radar I was one of the night lookouts. I swear some of the waves broke just below the bridge. It was OXO and toast all the way there. However, after completing the morning watch on radar I came out of the cabin amidships to find a lot of the ship's company hanging over the starboard side guardrails. Looking over the rail myself I saw that my shipmates were very busy ... pushing a floating mine off the ship's side with broom handles!

One Liverpudlian, who was also pushing the mine from the ship's side, remarked in earthy naval language: "I've heard of minesweeping, but this is ...ridiculous!"

When the floating mine had got far enough away from *HMS Vanity* the officers on the bridge believed they could blow it up using small arms fire. They failed, and the last I saw of it was floating out of sight into the morning mist. I believe we must have sailed through or very close to an enemy minefield.

By the way. Somebody did mention, in fairly strong matelot's terms, that nobody should strike the floating mine's horns with the broom handles.

Nobody did - otherwise I would not be relating this experience.

Geoffrey Barwell

Entombed

Fred Frost was a POW who became a forced labourer in a coal mine in Poland.

A couple of incidents (in the mine) very nearly had unfortunate results.

There was the occasion when I was sent, with a Polish labourer, to find some lengths of chain which had apparently been left in an old working. He had gone on ahead of me along the tunnel, each of us finding our way with our lamps. When I went to catch up with him he seemed to have disappeared.

So I continued to look for him holding my lamp in front of me. Eventually my light illuminated a blank coal face about 20 yards ahead. There was no other way he could have gone, so I went slowly forward unable to believe my eyes.

Then I stopped suddenly as there appeared, just in front of me, a great black hole about ten feet across. Obviously the ground had collapsed under him and he was then somewhere down in an old working.

Another couple of paces and I would have joined him without anyone having an idea where we had disappeared to.

I got as near to the edge as I dared and held my lamp over the hole to see if I could find out how far he had gone gown. Whether it was the lack of air or something else I don't know, but the lamp went out.

I was now in a very dodgy situation. How to find my way to another part of the mine where I could get help, in the pitch blackness and, on the way, crossing the avalanche of coal coming down the incline chute at the end of the passage? It was not going to be easy.

However, I inched my way along and managed to reach the incline leading up to the working on the higher level. It was quite a relief when I saw a miner's lamp shining up ahead. It was the Steiger, or shift supervisor, and having relit my lamp from his, I tried as well as I could to tell him what had happened.

Together we returned to the scene of the incident and, by passing a chain over the roof timbers and lowering it down into the hole between us, we were able to pull him out. He collapsed at our feet, badly shaken, but received little sympathy from, the German Steiger who told him to get up and get back to work.

It was certainly a near thing.

The other incident which one could call a near miss was when Roman and I were working at the coalface and the roof, a few yards behind us, came down cutting us off from our exit.

Fortunately we were able to dig a way over the fall assisted by someone from the other side.

To have been under so many tons of coal when the roof came down would have had dire consequences. It is no small wonder that there weren't more accidents as we were never given any instructions whatever regarding safety matters. It was just

Fred Frost. He was captured at Tobruk and survived forced labour in the mines of Silesia.

a case of learning by trial and error as one went along.

There was only one fatality that I heard of when, for some reason, the cage came down on a Polish worker who was for some reason in the pit shaft.

Fred Frost

Parting gifts

I was fortunate to be too young to be in the forces during WW2 but I volunteered in 1946 as a Regular soldier and served in the Royal Army Service Corps (RASC which became the Royal Corps of Transport and is now part of the Royal Logistics Corps).

Though I was not involved in WW2 I, nevertheless, saw active service since I was posted to Palestine during the trouble at that time until the land was handed to Israelis and the British Forces were evacuated.

Our company was one of the last to depart.

Because we had to use our transport and supply rations (food, POL, etc.) for all remaining British Forces still to evacuate, we were on the last ship to leave Palestine. The ship was due to sail, I believe, by 1800 hrs.

Unfortunately it did not leave for about two hours. We were told that divers were searching for a sten gun which had been "accidentally dropped in the water while a soldier was boarding." This was not true. It was known that limpet mines had been attached to the hull of the ship and set to explode while it was well out at sea.

That was my first lucky escape.

We landed at our destination, Tripoli, and were posted to a barracks which was once used by the Germans during the War.

We had not long been stationed there before it came up on orders that all personnel, with exceptions of persons on certain duties, would be available for cross-country running each Wednesday afternoon. Needless to say, I was one who was *never* on any "special duty" on Wednesdays. So, I was one of the company who had to go on this run. This went on for quite a few weeks.

Then, on Boxing Day, while we were in the barracks, there was a big explosion. It came from outside the barracks close to where we had been on our weekly cross-country run. Looking over the perimeter wall we saw the body of a local Arab. He had been blown to pieces.

Apparently he had found a German land mine which had been laid during the war years. The Royal Engineers were sent out to check the area and many other mines were discovered and destroyed.

Our route had been across a German minefield! There was no more cross-country running after that.

Henry Arthur Brooks

Wire

His back was a hell of a mess. It looked as if at some time he had had the "cat o' nine tails". I didn't like to ask how he got it and I knew that when Dad was ready he would tell me.

Every Saturday he would take me to whatever football match he had to referee. On this particular day it was at Nottingham Forest ground and it was a Cup round. The year was 1937 and I was about 12 years old.

He always got me a seat in the stand so I heard some of the remarks that were shouted, like: "Where's your guide dog ref.?" or "Borrow my glasses if you like ref.". In those halcyon days you seldom heard a swear word and, if anyone was foolish enough to start mouthing bad language, someone would soon put them in their place with remarks like: "Watch it mate! There's a youngster sitting there."

At the end of the game Dad would come and fetch me and take me down to the dressing rooms and introduce me to some of the players. I've shaken hands with some very good players, people like Stan Mortenson, Stan Matthews, Tommy Lawson, Nat Lofthouse, to name but a few. But there was only one man who really impressed me and that was the referee.

On this occasion my Dad was most keen for me to meet one of the linesmen who turned out to be one of his pals from the Coldstream Guards during the Great War. His name was Tom. Everyone in the changing room was in some form of undress or in the bath, there were no showers in those days. Tom said: "Has your Dad told you how his back got like that?"

Of course I said: "No."

This is what he told me.

"It was January 1917. We were in the front line. Some brainy General back in a posh Chateau, miles in the rear, decided that, as the ground was frozen solid, it would be a good time to capture the German trench in front of ours. Now, we'd got a friendly understanding with the Germans which we'd had with them all over Christmas and the New Year. 'If you don't shoot at us, we won't shoot at you.'

"As a result of our orders we had to get sufficient supplies of grenades and .303 ammunition to make our attack. Your Dad, who was platoon sergeant, took a limber to the ammo store some miles behind the lines with a couple of other men to help. He brought it back. A chain was formed and the unloading started. Well, we don't know what caused it, but all of a sudden there was this mighty explosion and everything disappeared in a great cloud . . . except for one body which sailed over our heads and landed on the wire about 50 yards to our front.

Fifteen men had gone in a flash. It was three days before we could make our attack, waiting for a new supply of ammunition.

As we went forward we were all keen to know who was the bloke on the wire. Well, it was your Dad! What's more, he was alive. But in a hell of a state.

"We took the German trench and five days later they took it back again. Three months later your dad appeared again to lead his old Platoon."

No wonder the referee impressed me so much.

Jeff Hollins

Deadly Decoy

Staney Sheasby has a much prized souvenir from his service at Tobruk, a small model of a Spitfire in light metal. In boring moments he used a nail file to create it from a piece of the wreckage of one of the dreaded Stukas which was shot down.

I was a despatch rider with the Home Guard. I was called up early in 1940 and joined the Royal Artillery HAA. It was just a few months later, while I was at a camp at Kinmel Bay, North Wales, that I heard that my brother Johnnie had been killed in an air raid on his RAF camp. I was able to attend the funeral.

In the early spring of 1941 the unit was sent to the Middle East and came under attack at Tobruk.

One of my jobs, with another soldier, was to man a dugout in the desert close to wooden decoy guns. Every time there was an air raid we had to get into this trench and pull a string to activate flash flares to give the impression that the wooden guns were firing at the Stuka bombers. The idea was that they would go for the wrong target. We were uncomfortably close to that target but fortunately we escaped injury.

Deadly decoy. Stanley Sheasby's job was to fire flares to trick enemy bombers into attacking decoy wooden guns.

I was one of ten or eleven drivers who managed to evacuate from Tobruk. We came under air attack constantly and we tried to take shelter from the Stuka dive bombers beneath a vehicle. I discarded my leather jacket in the desert because it shone in the moonlight and presented too good a target.

We reached Cairo eventually and encountered a 'Red Cap' military policeman who waned to lock us up, claiming we were drunk. When he heard that we had just come from Tobruk there were no further problems.

Earlier I caught typhoid and recovered. Then I developed an infected cyst on the chest and had nine operations before I embarked on a hospital ship for the UK in April 1943.

Stanley Sheasby

The Ju-87 Stuka suffered a mauling during the Battle of Britain, but it came into its own as a troop support aircraft in the desert and a machine for attacking shipping. Maximum speed: 217 mph; armament two fixed 7.9 mm machine guns firing forward from each wing and one machine gun mounted in the rear of the cockpit. The aircraft could carry one 1,110 lb. bomb and four 110 lb. bombs.

Chapter 7

Hush...hush!

Time and chance reveal all secrets.
18TH. CENT. PROVERB.

Japanese Morse

I was a radio operator with a Lancaster squadron based at Syerston in Nottinghamshire when The Mistake was made. My mate Wally volunteered for "special operators" in mistake for "special operations"!

But his biggest blunder was he had put my name down as well.

It was at a time when the RAF had more aircrew than aircraft. So I think they saw it as a glorious chance to ditch some of the dross.

We were sent post haste to join the Duke of Cornwall's Light Infantry at Bodmin for six weeks initiation into the Army way of life. From there we went to the Isle of Man where we joined 73 others, all ex-RAF, who also hadn't a clue what it was all about.

They made us sign the Official Secrets Act, gave us an exam, and promptly sent 10 back to where they came from. We didn't know if this was a result of the Official Secrets Act or if they had failed the exam.

Next day they let us into THE SECRET. We were to be trained as special operators to learn the Japanese Morse code (they have 790 letters not 26 like the more civilised countries) and we could then be put in a position where we could cause havoc behind the lines. We were thrilled to little moth balls by this information!

Now, to add to this, we had a PTI named Jack Fox. He was a Commando sergeant and ex-professional boxer. I was convinced he was out to kill us before the Japanese had a chance. The other thorn in our side was our orderly. Due to the fact that we were all sergeants we had one orderly between eight of us. He was ex-World War 1. His time expired after 25 years service just as Hitler got the new one going. I'm sure our orderly thought Hitler started the war as a personal vendetta against him.

His name was Carpenter, so naturally we called him "Chippy" to his face, but much worse behind his back. He was a walking beanpole but only about 5 ft. 2 ins. tall, and a face so full of hate for us that you couldn't tell whether he had just filled his trousers or he had just realised that someone had used one of his boots for a toilet.

This, of course, was mainly because he was only a Corporal after what was now 28 years of service; the other reason was because he hadn't a clue what we were doing.

His obsession was to try and find out. So we thought we would help a little . . . We set up a scheme. He was to be given bits of information when we "thought he couldn't hear". We had a 40 weeks course to do, so we had plenty of time.

My particular part was to say: "How the hell do they expect to keep our wimples on while we're dropping." This I duly did one morning while I was shaving and Wally was doing some revising, and we knew Chippy was outside the door.

The great day came. We passed our exams. Watch out Japs! At first I was stunned. Chippy came into my room and I swear he had tears in his eyes. He said: "I know I'm not supposed to know, but I've got a fair idea what you lot are up to and all I can say is you've got more guts than me. Best of luck."

For one horrible moment I thought he was going to kiss me.

This is what he had been fed . . .

We were a Commando group who were going to be dropped in France where the Germans had taken over a convent, kicked out the nuns, and replaced them with prostitutes dressed as nuns so that the local population wouldn't know. Our job was to drop in on them - also dressed as nuns - and to kill all the Germans!

I've often wondered if he ever tried to find out what happened to us.

The biggest joke of all was the fact that of the 34 of us who passed the final exam, I don't know of anyone who went to the Far East. Mind you, it did look a bit dodgy when the European war finished (I was in Italy at the time) and they started talking about shipping us out to the Far East.

I suppose it was because the Japanese heard we would be sent out that made them surrender.

Jeff Hollins

SOE Y Service

Patiently collecting all the necessary information about German codes, call signs, times of transmission, frequencies and conventions was the vital Y Service of the SOE. They were a very special body of men and women who lived isolated and lonely lives, constantly alert to the tiniest sound or change in their earphones.

In Britain they worked in innocuous sounding Home Defence Units, a title designed to appear no less secret than the Home Guard with which it was often confused - if people ever heard of it.

Operators from the Royal Signals were not allowed to share the Mess with their fellow soldiers and were usually given some bland cover story to disguise their activities.

Often they worked in foreign countries or in enemy held territory in conditions of great danger. They knew too much to be allowed to come back in the mainstream and receive the promotion they merited and deserved. Their families had no idea of their whereabouts and, even when the war was over, they were bound by their oath of security from disclosing the fact that they had held one of the most vital jobs in the war - because of it they were probably holding the same rank as the one in which they had begun . . .

Vicky Hollins

Secret Chinese tactics

At the bottom of a hill we were about to climb each prisoner was handed a slim green branch of a conifer type fir by a Chinese guard. These leafy branches we were ordered to carry over our shoulders and, during that day when aircraft were heard overhead, we sank to our knees, praying, with the green foliage covering our heads and most of our bodies.

So this was how the Chinese did it, advancing the length of Korea in daylight without being detected by the Air Force!

All along the mountain tops near the MSR (main supply route) Chinese soldiers were posted as air raid wardens in contact with one another all the way from the front to China.

When an aircraft was heard they would fire off their rifles shouting: "PEE YEN GEE". Then every vehicle would stop. Only when a further fusillade of shots and a blowing of whistles was heard would everyone move off again.

This worked very well in letting them know of approaching aircraft. You could hear the rifle shots getting closer and closer and you knew that aircraft would soon arrive. During the day the trucks stayed under cover in the numerous drive-in shelters by the side of the roads.

Henry O'Kane

A 'Stone Frigate'

On joining the Navy, after initial square bashing to knock us into shape, I was sent, with a number of others, for training as telegraphists, the instructors being GPO experts.

After three months of intensive instruction of reading and sending Morse for eight hours a day, and learning the procedures used by the enemy, we were finally examined and, on passing to the instructors' satisfaction, we were eventually designated Telegraphist Special Operators and duly drafted to various posts.

Mine was to the "Stone Frigate", known as *HMS Paragon* , at Scarborough. This was a land based Radio Station all constructed underground and with a compliment of 150 ratings, Wrens, and GPO officials all linked to radio sets and reading from a designated frequency, the aerials of which were linked to an aerial board and thence to two acres of aerials.

We read everything transmitted on our frequency and duly kept a record in a log. If a U-boat required to report he would come up on the frequency and transmit a short message which we were trained to recognise. We would then operate a foot switch and report through our mike our frequency which was then reported to HF/DF section who would alert other stations and read a bearing.

These bearings were duly collated and a position of the U-boat ascertained.

Some sets were used to read from stations which repeated messages for the benefit of ships at sea which could then check if they had missed any messages of importance to them.

When you read Morse for so many hours, particularly if you read the same station over a period of time, you become accustomed to the idiosyncrasies of the operators.

On this occasion I had been reading a repeat station, as they were called, from a French port when a message came up which had a U-boat prefix and was totally different in method to the operator I was reading.

Therefore I indicated the procedure for an HF/DF bearing after insisting that this was a U-boat and not a repeat message - bearings were taken and a position established. I was informed later that Coastal Command had caught a U-boat, obviously damaged, on the surface and making for a French port.

It was subsequently attacked and sunk. It had risked transmission so it would not be attacked by its own side as it entered harbour.

I know of no other case of a U-boat being destroyed by the intervention of a "Stone Frigate".

Ron Morley

Course fishing

When the war was over I had dreams of civvy street for us "hostilities only" servers. But the Navy had other ideas and I was attached to a destroyer, the *Zambezi*, to carry out some experiments. *(The Zambezi, 2,530 tons, was launched in November 1943 and scrapped in 1959.)*

You all know about depth charges used to try to cripple U-boats. Some of you know about torpedoes, an attack weapon fired from submarines and warships. Did you know that the torpedo is powered by a semi-diesel compressed air engine, a very large portion of the cigar shaped torpedo being a compressed air vessel?

The Navy decided to remove the engine and the air and replace them with TNT to make a very large depth charge. This would be fired from the torpedo tube, sink to a measured level, and then explode destroying any vessel within X miles.

The problem: How to fire the torpedo-depth charge without being blown out of the water! The answer: Go as fast as possible . . . and pray!

The site chosen for the experiment was the Kyle of Lochalsh in Scotland, which offered a good clear stretch of water which was easily controlled to keep out intruders for their own safety. A seismic vessel and instruments were placed in position on and around the Loch to measure the shock waves.

After preparing the tubes for firing my main task was the after switchboard. This controlled the electrics of the ship. As the *Zambezi* worked up to full speed, some 28-30 knots, I was to await a signal and then make my way to the forecastle, where as many of the crew as possible gathered, as the safest spot.

The "tin fish" was fired. As it exploded I was to run back aft to the switchboard to report and correct any damage that I could see.

The stern almost left the water with each explosion as we gathered up forward. Back aft almost all my switches were off; the ship was illuminated only by emergency lighting. Anything that could move had moved, with lots of breakages. After bringing all that we could back to normal we repeated the run - four times on our first day.

After the final run we put out the boats to pick up some of the stunned fish that littered the water. Boats appeared like magic from all round the shore. The local fishermen had a field day, all that they had to do was to pick up the fish.

On the fourth run of our second day we ran out of luck. The main drive shaft was bent and we could not possibly run at high speed. We limped across to Londonderry in Northern Ireland for repairs.

The Scottish fishermen were sorry to see us go.

After a week or so carrying out repairs, playing football with the locals and drinking porter, we set out across a very choppy Irish Sea, getting worse as it developed into a Force 10 gale. Bad enough. But when the Radar reported a faulty motor on the Radar mast, it got worse. With earphones, microphone and toolbag I had to climb the mast, strap myself on and carry out repairs. Then I had to synchronise the revolving aerial with the Radar boffins down below while swaying in a 20 ft. arc. Strangely enough I never noticed the sway until I had finished working.

Norman Schofield

SOE's secret stations

On commissioning John Stanfield was appointed to the 53rd (Welsh) Divisional Signals and joined at unit at Wem, Shropshire. In 1943, he was sent to India where he was given a GHQ posting to ME9 (Military Establishment).

ME9 was obviously the Secret Signals and the training centre for wireless operators to go behind enemy lines all over the East.

I found myself in Special Operations Executive (SOE) Force 136 training centre at Meerut. I was there prepared and trained to go to China and join Major Philip Smith as second in command SOE China Signals.

I learned a little about the special suitcase sets that were to be sent by various means behind the enemy lines. First the A3 and then the newer more powerful B2.

These were crystal controlled, working mainly from mains or six volt batteries. They worked great distances if the right frequencies were chosen. I also learnt the various ciphers and codes, the double transposition lower security, and the unbreakable one-time pads.

In Meerut there were wireless operators from many different eastern countries being trained to be sent, some by air drop, some by submarine, and any other way possible. Meerut was an old cantonment with a garrison church. There was a Methodist Chaplain, Varney and Mrs Varney, who were very welcoming.

After far too short a time learning about what I had unwittingly got into, urgent requests from Philip Smith meant that I was soon off to China.

First of all I had a long train journey to Calcutta where I had two nights in our Calcutta SOE Headquarters. It was a most humid place, practically 100%. Then to the airfield after going through customs. I had my bedding roll with as much as I could pack into it, and a tin trunk with all my other goods to follow.

As we went through customs we noticed a Chinese General being stripped of about four layers of clothing in which gold was packed. I wore my revolver as I was to do constantly for most of the next two years.

The plane was a Dakota, very much stripped down. There were aluminium bucket seats along each side. The trip was due to take six hours over the "hump" to Kunming in south west China. We stopped once at Dum Dum airfield to refuel. We had to go quite high, and there was no pressurising or oxygen. We landed at Kunming (6,000 ft.) a lovely area around a beautiful lake six or seven miles long and surrounded by mountains. This was the HQ of the American Air Force in China under General Clair Chenault.

The SOE Commanding Officer in Kunming was Colonel Kenny Brand, a delightful old China hand. The signal station was 15 miles out along the lake at Shi Shan where Philip Smith had set out our wireless station in the Church Missionary Society compound with the CMS hospital matron Miss Tindell. There were about 15 signals personnel living in the lower house and Philip and me in the small top house with the wireless room.

We had a motor cycle to take the signals into the Kunming Office. We also provided the communications for the Ministry of Economic Warfare (MEW) Office which was actually part of SOE and, through its undercover market deals, largely financed SOE world-wide. We also had a Jeep. We worked to India (Meerut and Calcutta) and up to Chunking, China's wartime capital, and down to the forward areas.

I was quickly on my way to our forward base at Kweilin, 400-500 miles down the road.

I was to take over the signals and officially be the Signals Officer for the British Army Aid Group (BAAG) originally formed to get prisoners out of Hong Kong as well as intelligence under Colonel "Doc" Ride. This was to be my cover.

The journey from Kunming took about four days by British Military Mission (BMM) truck. The roads were totally mud and stone and went through magnificent country and mountains. Kweilin was the American Air Force forward base. Airfields had been made between the extraordinary pepper pot hills that extended all over the region. My station worked to agents each side of Hong Hong and back to Kunming.

The Japs made a last attack down through the central cities from Changsha towards Kweilin. The Chinese tried to evacuate but there were far too many. Conditions were terrible. The one rail link back was completely inadequate, trains were very few and were incredibly overcrowded. It was hardly possible to see the train. People were slung under the carriages, roofs were packed, clinging to every part. I saw the last train depart and it was almost invisible.

The Americans blew up the airfields. The electric power was cut and we had to work the wireless sets from batteries and try to keep them charged. We would have to retreat but our BMM trucks were very decrepit and had to run on wood alcohol.

I had great problems in keeping the wireless going and went in the truck to the American airfield to see if I could salvage a battery. The American Air Force was blowing up a lot of stores and I was very lucky to get an enormous accumulator, fully charged, and also half a drum of air plane oil to keep our trucks going.

The Chinese evacuated and burned the city. I watched the city burning and the explosions of the scorched earth policy during the night before we left for Yishan. Just before we left we managed to get an A3 set down to Hong Kong area to watch the Hong Kong harbour traffic.

Our transports were old BMM trucks which had originally come over the Burma road. The Chinese drivers knew nothing of mechanics. The trucks ran on wood alcohol which was better than the Chinese trucks which generated gas from a charcoal burner in the back into a gas bag on the roof.

My truck was very difficult to start and all the lights, except one side light, did not work. The truck was almost impossible start. In the morning we had to light a fire under the engine to warm it up with a little petrol to prime it. When the engine started the accelerator spring went. We could accelerate, but not decelerate! So we had to tie a string to the pedal and pull it back each time. The fuel pump gave up so the only way was to put the tank on the roof of the cab to work by gravity.

At Yishan my wireless station was set up in a graveyard half a mile away from HQ. It was just a lath and plaster hut. My Chinese operators worked up to Kunming and Kweiyang and down to the agents near Hong Kong.

The conditions were terrible, as far as sanitation and health were concerned, with thousands of refugees.

Rumours of Jap advances made everyone jittery. Our explosives experts mined several bridges and did some demolition work for the Chinese. We retired further up the road to Dushan, about 200 miles back.

My problem for the retreat was to keep the agents in touch. I spent long hours on cipher messages to Kunming and the agents to ensure that messages could be passed from Hong Kong area, and to them, without a gap when we were on the road to Kunming. Frequencies and times were essential. Finally, we went back with the rest of the BAAG to Kweiyang where the BMM liaison officer, Major Gould, had a set up.

Finally, we pulled back to Kunming. This was a tremendous trip over very primitive roads. One spectacular hill had 27 hairpin bends all the way up. Back in

Shi Shan our wireless station beside the Kunming lake was sited under the magnificent Western Hills with the wonderful rock temple high up in the hills overlooking the lake.

During this time a catastrophe took place when our despatch rider "lost Indo China." We were working agents in Indo China for the French and the French were rapidly being swamped by the Japs and urgently asked for supply drops. The American Air Force had agreed to provide planes and were standing by for a message from the Indo China agents to give a place and time. Nothing arrived and the French officer kept asking as it was essential to go before the moon vanished.

After a search the message, which should have gone to Kunming, was found in the wrong page of the dispatch book. The moon had gone and no drop was possible.

It was about then that Philip went to India and was ordered to hand over China Signals to me. He was away for about six weeks. When he returned I was to go north to be Signals Officer for North China with the Chinese Director of Military Intelligence (DMI). I was to go when suitable transport was available. In fact I had half an hour's notice to fly to Chunking. Chunking airfield was on a sand bank in the middle of the river and, as the hills on each side rose several thousand feet, it was often impossible to land. However, all went well.

I was to go with Mr Ho (General, Chinese Intelligence) and Adrian Evans (Captain Intelligence) by truck with my Signals Corporal Best, who was to train and oversee the Chinese wireless operators to work on our B2 suitcase sets. In our BMM truck and a Jeep we set off for Sian, via Chengdu. It took about four days.

Chengdu is a very ancient city and, in the vast plain, there is the most sophisticated water and irrigation system, about 2,000 years old. We set off north under the foothills of the Himalayas, a magnificent journey. Eventually we reached Sian, this old capital of China of many dynasties. During the Han dynasty, from 200 BC, this was the greatest city in the world with about 2-million inhabitants..

We set up the wireless sets to work back to Chunking. My watch, bought in Durban, was the only accurate time available and we arranged for the first schedule on the time fixed. We had tremendous face when, dead on time, Chunking came in. We could hear their signals all over the compound.

My next job was to establish wireless stations each side of the Yellow River bend.

The Japanese occupied the other side of the Yellow River. These were strategic points where agents could cross the river with information about Japanese movements. If the agents had to walk to deliver the information it would be totally out of date.

The stations were to be called "Sparrow" and "Crow". I had also got two walkie talkies, just produced, so that the agents could speak across the river. The Yellow River is a vast river, even a thousand miles inland, it was miles across.

The diary of my trip, as I tried to keep it going, had to be a bit circumspect. There was a $10,000 reward by the Japs on the head of any allied officer. This was

An innocuous looking hut became the ears of the SOE in China. John Stanfield (l) at the wireless station at Yinshan, on the Yellow River, in 1944.

the first time I had a personal body guard which was often a nuisance and an embarrassment.

The Jeep and trailer were filled up with stores for two wireless stations and a drum of petrol as well as our bedding rolls. The party consisted of Mr Ho Kan Tzen (General), myself, and Guo (Ho's secretary and honorary Colonel), Lai Ping Kuen (my W/T mechanic), two Chinese wireless operators (Chinese Captains), and Chinese servant Lai.

I had two complete wireless stations with batteries, steam and hand-worked battery chargers, a drum of fuel, and all our bedding. It was a good load.

Tuesday June 26, '45. We were booked to be off on Monday June 25. The Jeep and trailer left by train on Sunday for the railhead. We went to the station by rickshaw where, under Mr Ho's wing, we had a first class compartment to ourselves.

The train left a 1730. Food was produced on the train. It was old first class rolling stock, very comfortable. It only ran about a hundred miles.

We followed the Wei river through the very dry planes with innumerable grave mounds shown up by the setting sun, including the vast tomb mound of the first Emperor.

70

(It was guarded by 6,000 full-size terracotta buried warriors which were not discovered until 1974).

This area is one of the cradles of the human race. On our right was the famous mountain Wha Shan. Eventually we arrived at Wha Yin, in the Yellow River bend where the Jeep and trailer were waiting. If we had carried on we would have had to change into an armoured train, past the Jap positions in the bend We spent the night in a small hotel. I had borrowed the British Naval Attache's small safari camp bed which was most useful.

Wednesday June 27 '45. Usual trouble with drivers. Found the spare wheel deflated, and two of the other wheels soft. Also five gallons of petrol missing - I would like to shoot the bloke . . . also no pump. Finally we decided that we would have to push on to the rail head, seven of us on the Jeep with the wireless operator.

We started off on the most tremendous drive I have ever done. I only managed to get into top gear once. The "road" was six inches deep in most parts with dust, and worse up the hills. Along the flat I had to go in second or bottom and up the hills I was lucky to get up in low ratio. On one hill I stalled in double low ratio, practically unheard of in a Jeep that is said to be able to climb a house in double bottom.

Dust settled in clouds and, at times, we were completely blinded. The road was mostly in a cutting with the only firm spots right on the sides. If I got on the firm spot I could go along in bottom, otherwise it was bottom low ratio. It was just like ploughing. Nothing without four wheel drive would have had a hope. Unfortunately the low gear used up three times as much gas as we had bargained for.

Dykes had been cut across the road for irrigation. How the Jeep made it I do not know. The bumps were terrific. At times I wondered why the Japs didn't have a pot at us. There were two water crossings, one a boat bridge and one a decrepit ferry.

Finally we were welcomed to the village nearest to "Sparrow" with a deputation. We scraped off the dust and proceeded.

The arrival at "Sparrow" was terrific, two miles through a gorge with soft bottom, needing double low gear. Enough said. The whole village was lined up to greet us, all the children. The village had suffered considerably from shelling. Put up the aerial and tried to function at 1800 sked (wireless schedule), no answer. Extraordinarily poor village and most of the income derived from smuggling across the Yellow River from the Japs.

Three agents were introduced to us after a meal in the guest house. Seem to be pretty stout fellows. The guest house has plenty of marks where shells fell. The guest house consists of two rooms and a hall. The so-called lavatory is across the street. Head of Office Chien and Chief of Staff Tsai. We walked around the village and to the watch tower overlooking the Yellow River and the Jap lines.

At that time I must have been the furthest British soldier not in captivity.

Thursday, June 28, '45. Up for the 8.00 sked, still no luck. Meal at 11am. Curious that I am not hungry with only two meals a day. Fixed steam generator . . . looks like a little toy steam engine, the boiler had to be fuelled by the residue of the cotton crop. Walked around the town and introduced to two men who were to take the walkie talkies across the river. I tried to explain the workings to them.

Breakfast/lunch at 11 am. This was a feast in our honour. A slow afternoon, the Chinese operator tested the wireless without my knowledge and obviously made a mess of it. To climax the day, came the 1800 sked. I got the time by a tremendously loud Pacific BBC transmission. The first quarter hour was no good, then I made a desperate cast to a low harmonic which we heard strength 5. The Sian station operator then suddenly went into a harmonic not even on the signal plan and about two miles above anything possible. Of course that was the finish.

A battery charging competition was arranged with the hand generator, in the firelight. Every agent had a go and between the lot raised the specific gravity of the battery from 1180 to 1190! I cannot think they will be prepared to turn the generator by hand for 3-4 hours every day.

Back to the guest house, we sat talking till 11 pm and listening to the machine guns on the other side.

Friday June 29, '45. Up early for the sked. Everything finally came right and I got through on the two frequencies I had told them. This allows us to get off. I was very worried about rain clouds. If it had rained I would have had as much hope of getting the Jeep or any vehicle in the world back as climbing Mount Everest by Jeep.

The village saw us off, a slightly lighter load, with one station less. But the bumps still terrific.

The drive back was a bit better as we were lighter, but it was very tiring as I did all the driving. We went along the side of the river, but, as it was cloudy, the Japs could not see us properly. Back to the railhead where we saw our military friends.

Off to Wha Yin. A good trip but a following wind and colossal dust. Finally into an inn and wash and safari bed where I am writing this. Rain, very cool. Only just made it.

Saturday June 30, '45. Late up . . a couple of peaches for breakfast and a gentle stroll to the station with the famous Wha Shan (flowery mountain) on our left magnificently clear after the rain. Two little children ran up to me and solemnly bowed, they had obviously been told to be polite to foreigners.

We met the train and found that only ten gallons of petrol had been sent. We have a minimum of good roads which are unlikely to be with us. Finally I went to an American OSS (equivalent to SOE) who was running a little wireless station. He gave me as much petrol as I wanted.

Sunday July 1, '45. Away by 9 am to establish "Crow". Glorious morning. We crossed the Wei river on a pontoon bridge and arrived in Ta Li in good time the road being quite good although mud patches were difficult. From there to Hoping. A good deal of low gear work in thick mud patches. Hoping to Hencheng were the worst bits. This is where I stalled going up quite a steep hill in double bottom. I yelled for them all to get off and push after putting blocks under the wheels. Terrific gorges. Into Hancheng at 7 pm, a most attractive town, good streets with trees. Welcomed and light food until the meal. Quite a feast . . . then to the bath house where we were scrubbed and foot massaged.

After returning the agent arrived with Jap papers. I was given the best room. It has good maps and pins showing the agents' lines of communication.

Monday July 2, '45. 0700 heard Eagle (Sian) on low frequencies, but lost him when testing others.

We went for a ride in the Jeep to the Yellow River, five kilometres, where there is a small village. This is the best place to get across this immense river, a good mile.

Just as we arrived a company of guerrillas had just crossed with a Jap sword and some rails. We walked down the cliff path to the river. Some Americans are functioning across the river . We heard gun fire on the other side. Saw boats with stark naked boatmen, burnt almost black by the sun. The Captain, who controls the crossings, entertained us to water melons and Jap cigarettes, exact imitation of WD & HO Wills.

Back and rest. The wireless still unhappy. No contact 1200 or 1400. Other end will not ask us to transmit on another frequency. Slept most of the afternoon. Invited to dinner by the local General at 5 pm. Usual sea slugs! I am almost getting resigned, I might even eat them if there was nothing else. Still no wireless contact.

Tuesday, July 3, '45. 0700 sked today, thank goodness. Packed and off. The driver took the Jeep out of the town and we had a mile to walk. Then I drove. Up the few very steep hills, but with a lighter load as both wireless stations established, the Jeep managed well.

After establishing "Sparrow" and "Crow" on the Yellow River I returned to Sian. The wireless links were working well, forward from the agents and back to Chunking. There were big plans being formed to create a guerrilla force to work behind the Jap lines. Colonel Bridge and I went to see the War Zone Commander, Marshal Hu Zung Nan, in his HQ to plan the guerrilla army.

John Stanfield

By August 8, Major Stanfield heard that the atomic bombs had been dropped on Japan and he was free to visit and explore the historic area which had been occupied by many dynasties from the first Emperor Quin Shi Whang in the 4th century BC.

Chapter 8

Life Behind the Wire

"For you, the war is over . . ."

I love a brave soldier who has undergone the baptism of fire.
NAPOLEON BONAPARTE (1817)

'For you, the war is over.'

The time came for me to return to Tobruk.

I got a lift with a convoy going to Cairo along the coast road. I had gone off the idea of returning by the train on which I came. I was soon back in the old routine wondering really why I had ever been sent on the course.

Much to my surprise a few days later I was sent for by the Adjutant who informed me that my name had been put forward for the next course which was to be held *in England.* It took quite a while for this to sink in. The thought of suddenly being shipped or even flown home was beyond belief. But my hopes were rather short lived.

Apparently Rommel's Afrika Korps had different ideas. By now the Eighth Army was in retreat and eventually Tobruk was surrounded.

Our position was close to the Derna-Tobruk road and, from the middle of June, we had waved goodbye to a steady stream of convoys heading east until, at last, the road was cut and we were left with the prospect of being involved in another siege.

On June 20 (1942) German tanks came over the escarpment. Our anti-aircraft guns became anti-tank guns until we were overrun. Orders came for us to try to make it to the beach harbour where, I suppose, there could have been the possibility of getting away. Unfortunately our truck was shot up and I finished in the Beach Field Hospital, a collection of tents by the shore.

My injuries were not too serious though I had lost the use of my legs when I landed on my back near the truck.

The following morning, lying on stretchers in the tent, a German officer with his retinue appeared through the open flap and informed us that, "For you, the war is over." Needless to say he received an appropriate reply from the occupants of the stretchers. We were visited by a Canadian MO who gave instructions that I was to be put on a mattress on a flat board. He thought I had a fractured pelvis. At the same time part of a bullet was removed from my right instep.

It would be about the beginning of August when I awoke one morning and looked out through the open tent flap and saw a white painted ship with a large red cross on the side riding at anchor just off the beach. There was great speculation about whether we would be evacuated; if so, where to. Would it be Italy or Germany?

Later that morning our Canadian MO came round, in the company of two or three German members of the Afrika Korps, to decide which of us should go on stretchers and which could walk. I expected to go on foot but the MO put me down as a stretcher case.

Then one of the Germans who could speak some English apologised to us for having to hand us over to the Italians. Later on it became pretty evident that the German-Italian alliance was rather tenuous among the troops on the ground. I didn't have much trouble in packing ready to leave. My personal possessions I carried in my pockets and, in addition, I held on tightly to my greatcoat and water bottle.

The orderlies carried my stretcher out to a waiting field ambulance and, along with several other cases, set off bumping over the rough ground towards the coast.

The hospital ship was out in the harbour several hundred yards away and the thought crossed my mind that getting from where I was lying out to the ship, and then up on the deck, could pose a problem. There then appeared a floating platform with a small wheelhouse and an engine. This chugged up to the quayside and three or four of us were lifted up and placed on the platform. Away we went out to the ship and came alongside.

From my position lying on my back the side of the ship just towered away from me. How on earth was I going to get up on to the deck?

The answer came as a sort of crane jib swung out from the ship and lowered a cradle, oval in shape, about the size of a bath, down on to the platform.

I was lifted on my stretcher and lodged on the top of this cradle. The signal was given and I was lifted into the air and, as I hung on tightly, I was swung out over the water and then back in over the ship and deposited with a bump on the deck.

It was an experience I would not care to repeat too often! The whole operation seemed most precarious. I was then picked up and taken down a steep flight of stairs to the deck below. Here there were rows of double bunks on to one of which I was deposited and left to size up the situation from my lofty perch.

Having surveyed this for a little while I decided that I must do a little exploration, mainly to try to find something to eat and drink. The possibility of being fed and watered on my bunk seemed remote. Not without a little difficulty I climbed down to the deck and joined the others moving around.

Neither friend nor foe seemed interested in my existence so I wandered around until I found a drinking water tap which proved quite refreshing. Then I came upon a small sort of messroom in which several men sat around a table eating something or other. They were mainly Italians who took no notice of me as I sat down with them and helped myself to a bowl of macaroni and a second bowl containing some rather rough vino.

That evening I got myself to the upper deck where, much to my surprise, there was a cinema show in progress. Seeing one or two vacant seats in the three or four rows of chairs I sat down next to a German member of the Afrika Korps to watch the film. It transpired that neither of us was particularly interested in the entertainment although I was somewhat surprised when he turned to me and addressed me in excellent English.

He told me of his time spent in England before the war and how he was just as fed up as we were with this war in the North African desert. We got on well together as, at the time, we were on neutral ground, as it were.

Fred Frost

Some 33,000 Allied troops, 19,000 of them British, were captured at Tobruk. Rommel received some 2,000 tons of much needed petrol as well as 5,000 tons of provisions and 2,000 serviceable vehicles.

Guards protected us from angry civilians

We all bailed out over the sea, but drifted on to the coast in the vicinity of Honfleur. Shortly after 3 am we all landed in the neighbourhood of Honfleur and were eventually captured and later taken to Le Havre in an American truck!

We were detained at a 'drome NE of the town and later taken to Paris by rail. We were obviously dangerous customers judging by the number and armament of the guards!

We travelled first class, luckily for me with small but very painful injuries to the face, head and leg. I was examined at Le Havre by the Luftwaffe doctor who thought I may have a rupture and asked me to cough!

Many folk in Paris gave us a sly "V" and thumbs up sign and one old gentleman proudly lifted his silk top hat to us. Le Havre folk were not so friendly disposed, a fact which I could not but help appreciate when we were herded through the town later.

From Paris we travelled to Frankfurt by rail on hard wooden seats. The night journey seemed endless.

I had my first view of the Rhine - from ground level - and saw something of the Rhine valley. The scenery was lovely though hardly appreciated on an empty tummy, no sleep, and other things.

A man on Frankfurt station incited the crowd against us. Perhaps he had lost a son in the war. Extra guards came to protect us and the crowd dispersed. Our Luftwaffe guards were pretty reasonable and most of them treated us as fellow humans. Frankfurt is a lovely town. We walked through it to the tram-cum-train stop and boarded the strange contraption en route for Dulag Luft.

Eric Herwin

Brainwashing prisoners

Henry O'Kane was a prisoner of the Chinese for two and a half years after being captured in Korea during the heavy fighting on the Imjin River. The

Chinese made sustained efforts to indoctrinate prisoners with Communist culture.

About 46,000 Britons, including many National Servicemen, fought under United Nations command in Korea between 1950 and 1953. Britain lost 1,078 men. Some 1,036 British POWs were repatriated and another 31 are believed to have died in captivity. It is claimed that about 100 are still missing, unaccounted for.

Each platoon had a political instructor who spoke a brand of English. Our instructor was a Chinese called Su, but he was known by all and sundry as "Machine Gun" because of his brand of the English spoken word.

He once told me that his father was a rich landlord in China but that after the Revolution he had seen the "error of his ways" and joined the People's Party. Like the rest of the political staff Su was well educated and he was a lecturer in astronomy at Peking University.

He was devout and dedicated and serious in his indoctrination and he truly believed he was doing us all a great favour in bringing to us the teaching of the Communist leaders, Stalin, Lenin and Mao Tse-Tung, who were his heroes.

Other political instructors with whom I came into contact were all well-educated mature Chinese. All were fanatical Communists and, like Su, were all known to us prisoners by the nicknames with which we tagged them.

The Chinese began forced study in earnest.

The basic means of indoctrination was a lecture, sometimes four hours in length, and eventually a group discussion.

Attendance at all lectures was compulsory, even the sick had to attend and, as the disciplinary rules and regulations of Camp 1. observed "everybody must be serious and in orderly manner. The bad behaviours of disobedient, free action, making noises, joking and dozing, are strictly forbidden."

We spent hours on the square attending long lectures on the manifesto of the Communist party, political economies, the writings of Marx, Engels, Lenin and the thoughts of Mao. Then we had lectures at company level, then at platoon level, and later after discussion, in our rooms, we had to make notes on paper which we had to submit to the political instructors.

From time to time we were made to undergo written examinations designed to see whether we understood the points made in the lectures and could reproduce them.

Then the questioning and the interrogation began. Daily, men would be taken away to be interrogated at the various HQ levels. The questions were always much the same and the records were strictly kept by the Chinese political instructors.

"Who started the Korean War?"

"Why did the US send troops to Korea?"

"What did you think of the the Wall Street Imperialists?"

"What do you think of the Chinese Communists?"

"What is your opinion of the 'peace loving' people?"

"What do you think about the War?"

"What is life like in Britain?"

"What property do you own?"

"What is your father's income?"

"What is your grandfather's occupation?"

"What is your religion?"

"Do you vote?"

"What do you think of Sygman Rhee?"

"What do men talk about amongst themselves?"

From time to time I was subjected to this type of harassment and the same type of questioning. Looking at these questions now they appear laughable and unreal, as indeed they were then. But, to the Chinese political instructors, it was all a very serious business

When called upon to answer such questions the replies depended entirely on one's attitude or indeed one's state of health on a particular day. Days when I felt rebellious and truthful I would answer the first question which was nearly always: "Who started the Korean War?", by saying: "North Korea." Needless to say this caused quite a controversy. Days when I felt subdued and beaten I would come up

Henry O'Kane, the POW who Chinese captors tried to 'brainwash'.

with the answer required: "South Korea." This would usually produce a smile of understanding and a cigarette.

It was a very dangerous game. The Chinese had a "lenient policy" that worked only under certain rules. If these rules were not followed closely it was easily forgotten. At these interrogation sessions emphasis would often be put on the word "confess." "Confess to war crimes." After all we were all supposed to be war criminals.

Sometimes I argued that I saw the Chinese shoot up ambulances full of wounded men and surely that was an atrocity that showed lack of respect for the Red Cross. But this was something they always denied, claiming that *I* was the war criminal.

I was never brave enough to bring up the fact that I knew that Chinese troops, not North Koreans, had shot prisoners captured at Happy Valley. I also knew that men of the RUR (Royal Ulster Regiment) Battle Patrol, as well as Royal Engineers, were shot out of hand at the Imjin River.

Knowing all this was always at the back of my mind. Prisoners *did* disappear in North Korea. I knew it could happen again and most of these facts, as well as other deaths of Britons, were later proved at a UN Atrocities Commission in New York after the Armistice.

The Chinese worked on the assumption that the best way to snare a group of prisoners was to give them a guilt complex and then to lead them to self-denunciation, self-betrayal and self-criticism.

If the Chinese political instructors had been students of human nature they would have realised that with most prisoners they were on a loser from the start.

Henry O'Kane committed the ultimate crime in Chinese eyes. While on a work party, moving heavy logs from the hills, he let a pile of 20-foot logs roll downhill and they flattened a grain crop. He was paraded through local villages and handed over to Korean policemen and thrown into the local jail. He shared a stinking cell with four Americans and the enemy, three Communist soldiers who had transgressed.

I was sitting cross-legged next to an American, a corporal in the US Marines. In snatched phrases of whispered conversation I was to learn the rules of the place.

No talking. We were to squat cross-legged from dawn to dusk, to sit straight up and we were not allowed to lean back against the wall as this brought the wrath of the guards.

At six o'clock that evening our food arrived. Rough sorghum, (soya bean meal) a dirty tin bowl each three times a day with a dirty communal bowl of drinking water. The same sorghum and water came at six o'clock, twelve o'clock and six o'clock daily. After each meal we were allowed to visit the latrine which was next to our cell. These were the only visits allowed.

At night we lay on the bare wooden floor huddled together in our misery. All I had to wear was the once white cotton shorts that I had on when I was brought to the jail. The climate in North Korea was such that on hot sunny days it was oppressive, but the nights were long and cold. So, there we were, stretched out on the floor of our cell in the far north of Korea. Four men in the Army of the United Nations and three from the Communist enemy, united together as prisoners.

We clung together for warmth. Filthy, dirty, unshaven and bruised black and blue crawling with lice which lived in the floorboards, we awaited the dawning of a new day.

One morning the jailer ordered me out and I found Machine Gun and Ding had arrived. Machine Gun gave me a long lecture on the error of my ways, urging me to confess. He went away. On his way out Ding gave me part of my ration of tobacco.

By this time I was ready to write down anything about my crime. But I was left to think about it for another 24 hours before Machine Gun returned with a pencil and paper.

I had no doubt about what I had to do. I had destroyed the crops which had belonged to the "peace loving" people. It was one of the toughest crimes in the book.

I covered the paper given to me with all the Communist phrases I could think of, made all the promises, and gave it to Machine Gun when he returned 24 hours later. In the back of my mind I knew that the Chinese would not accept the first written confession. I would have to repeat it verbatim. This I did every other day.

Every day I stank a bit more. There were no washing facilities. The lice crawled out of the floorboards. It must have been the only boarded floor in Chong-Song.

Finally the day arrived when Machine Gun accepted my confession and criticism. Ding arrived and escorted me from the Korean jail. When we got outside Ding indicated I should walk in front of him. After a few steps I turned round and found Ding was following me with his nose covered. I must have really stunk!

He escorted me to the river where I had a wash and then he escorted me, dripping, towards Company HQ. I was quite surprised at my progress - I felt weak. On my return to the squad hut I had a further wash with bowls of hot water and finally a shave.

That evening I appeared before the assembled members of 7 Coy. and all the Chinese from Company HQ. I was to criticise myself and receive my sentence, fourteen days hard labour.

In my wandering years that followed I have often been aware of a smiling Chinese interrogator sitting by my bed in some hazy awakening moment. On others, the bad ones, the Immu Gun have been climbing in the windows. But that is all gone now.

Henry O'Kane

I tried to eat the message!

When dawn was breaking on Monday, May 28, 1940, I left the headquarters of 143 Infantry Brigade on a borrowed motor bike.

It was fortunate, for my own peace of mind, that I did not know that on the previous day, 20 miles to the south-east, at Le Paradis, an SS Regiment had lined up against a barn and shot 97 prisoners, mostly from the Royal Norfolks, or that within a few hours, 25 miles to the north-west at Esquelbecq, another SS unit would double march some 60 men of the 2nd Battalion of my own Regiment - the Royal Warwickshires - into a barn and bomb and machine gun them.

My own experience of German front line troops was to be rather different.

Two days earlier 143 Brigade had been lent to 5th Division and diverted to fill a gap in the Allied line, along a dry canal between Ypres and Comines, caused by the retreat northwards of the disintegrating Belgian Army.

A captured enemy plan had shown that the German Sixth Army was about to launch an attack westwards to link up with their armoured thrust which had already reached the Channel Coast and was threatening the ports of Calais and Dunkirk. Thus, they would cut off the main part of the BEF and large elements of the French Army still south of the river Lys.

The three battalion Brigade, with 1/7th Royal Warwicks on the left, 8th Royal Warwicks in the centre and 1st Ox. and Bucks. on the right, had taken up positions during May 26 between the villages of Houthem and the river Lys at Comines.

The first Germans arrived in the late afternoon and a heavy attack was launched at dawn with three divisions against the one British 5th Division. Vicious fighting took place all day during which 143 Brigade, as well as 13th and 17th Brigades, on their left, were pushed back several hundred yards, but held.

Counter-attacks during the late evening of May 27, by three companies of Royal Engineers, a company of 6th Black Watch, and 3rd Bn. Grenadier Guards, and 2nd Bn. North Staffords, drove the enemy back to the canal line.

By the early hours of May 28 the Brigade's task was virtually completed and tens of thousands of British and French troops had passed behind on their way to the coast.

The commander 143 Brigade called a conference to issue orders for a controlled withdrawal. The liaison officer from 3rd Grenadier Guards failed to turn up and I was called in to act in his place. As the meeting broke up the Brigade Major said to me jokingly: "Don't forget Denis, if you are captured, eat it!"

There was no direct road through the sector through which the Guards had attacked and no one knew exactly where they had set up their headquarters. I found the Guards RAP (Regimental Aid Post) and was given directions. I proceeded down the main road, along which 1st Ox and Bucks had withdrawn, intending to turn left along a side road. I missed the turn and rode too far.

I did not know that the attacking units had already withdrawn from the canal or that the Germans had not followed them up. Hence, there was a wide no-man's-land. I had not seen a soul since I left the RAP until I saw two Germans - probably part of a probing patrol. I braked and jumped.

They fired. I landed in the roadside ditch with two smashed legs and then spent much of an interesting but painful day watching the world go by.

The first thing I thought of was the Brigade Major's remarks. I opened my haversack and tried to eat the message. No hope! I tore it into small pieces which I stuffed into the mud in the ditch. The Germans had gone. I went through the contents of the haversack which included a leather wallet with a photograph of my fiancée.

Suddenly, down the road from the direction from which I had come, came a group of civilians whose hamlet had changed hands twice already and who must have thought, correctly, that it would soon be fought over again. A teenage girl made to come over to my assistance but her terrified father dragged her away. I met her 55 years later to thank her. She said I hadn't changed!

Next a British carrier *(Bren Gun Carrier)* from 6th Black Watch, which had come up in the morning to occupy the line abandoned by 1st Ox and Bucks, appeared. One of the crew took up a covering position with the Bren gun and the other two came over to pick me up. Before they reached me a shell hit the carrier and it started to burn. The three men made off at speed!

Shortly afterwards, a German section came up the road and followed them. After a while a single German came back, waved to me, and disappeared towards Comines. He returned, and in due course the whole section came back. One moved me into a more comfortable position, another picked up the photo, no doubt thinking it was a map case. Then he threw it up the road as if playing ducks and drakes. They all proceeded back to Comines.

Time passed and a medical orderly appeared and put a dressing on my thigh. He went off. Later still a gefreiter *(Lance Corporal)* and two men arrived with a stretcher. Skillfully and tenderly they put me on the stretcher. The gefreiter saw the photo and went over and picked it up. He asked who it was, put it on my chest, and it is on my desk now. I was taken across fields and put down by the canal where a heavy mortar section was in action.

I was then taken to a barn which was full of British and German wounded. A German doctor came over. Before examining me he shook hands - an unexpected action, but I discovered 30 years afterwards that he had been a Regimental MO in the same area in 1914 when he had attended a wounded Grenadier officer. They had exchanged addresses and had become firm friends in the inter-war years. The doctor had already attended wounded guardsmen and had discovered that his friend's son was only a few hundred yards away. He was in fact Adjutant of 3rd Grenadier Guards, the very man I had been looking for a few hours before.

All this had taken most of the day and it was dusk when I was put in an ambulance with three Germans and moved to a modern Belgian hospital at Courtrai which had been commandeered.

There I received good treatment for four days before being transferred to a school and then, in my bed, on a horse-drawn cart over the Lys on a raft, for the bridges had been blown, to a civilian hospital staffed by Sisters of the Sacred Heart.

There I had a foot amputated and was nursed with loving care. I was visited daily, against German orders, by lovely Belgian ladies. This lasted for three months until, one day, Germans arrived and found the ward full of visitors. I was moved, first to Ghent, and then in November 1941 to a hospital in Dieburg, south of Frankfurt.

After many more moves I was repatriated through Sweden in October 1943.

It is interesting to note that not a single item of my possessions was taken from me and that, even when I was repatriated, I was given a note signed by a German paymaster certifying that he held the Mark equivalent of the English, Belgian and French coins found in my pockets when my trousers were removed.

The British paymaster credited me with the Sterling equivalent. This, in the middle of a world war!

Denis Dodd

A year in chains

Stalag V111b. Oct. 6, 1942. Told on parade this morning that all Red Cross supplies, all schooling, and all entertainments are stopped as a reprisal for the ill-treatment of German POWs in Britain!

The reprisals were probably in response to the Dieppe raid. *(The Allied disaster was on August 18-19, 1942, in which 1,000 died on the beaches, 550 were wounded and 2,000 Canadians were captured by the Germans).* Afterwards two or three German soldiers who had been captured and had their wrists bound, were drowned when the landing craft taking them back to England was sunk and the bodies washed back on to the French coast. RAF POWs at V111b (Lamsdorf) were later to suffer the consequences.

It was on October 7, 1942 that the German High Command threatened that, because German prisoners captured at Dieppe and Sark were bound, all British Prisoners taken at Dieppe would be put in chains from October 8. The same day the British Government announced that if the German threat was carried out a like number of German prisoners would be manacled and chained. This, they said, would become effective from 12 noon on October 10 unless the British prisoners were released.

Two days later, on October 9, the German high Command threatened to fetter three times the number of prisoners similarly treated by the British. Winston Churchill told the House of Commons on October 13 about the Government's protest and gave an assurance that if the enemy desisted the British would withdraw counter-measures at once.

Oct. 10, 1942. All RAF personnel bound with Red Cross string at the wrists this morning and unbound late afternoon. It is awkward having to exist with bound hands but it could be a hundred times worse. Told we had been released temporarily on the orders of the Fuhrer! Some chaps got a hiding today but it's not too bad if one adopts a low profile.

During this period of "strafe" we were guarded by 30 or 40 German soldiers. To be caught unbound was to invite a beating though not all the guards felt happy about tying us up - some would tie so tightly it would stop the circulation and others were humane. However a Feldwebel (Senior NCO) was always in attendance to ensure that we were well secured. It was the use of Red Cross string which upset us as much as anything.

Oct. 11, 1942. Wrists bound but will write to Iris. Am learning to do almost anything whilst bound up. It is rather monotonous all the same, especially attending to one's toilet.

Oct. 16, 1942. Our sixth day of being bound up. When I get back to England I shall walk about with my hands in front of me!

Oct. 18, 1942. Shaving with my hands tied is becoming fairly simple.

Oct. 19, 1942. About 60 RAF chaps arrived last night from Dulag Luft. They were unhappy to see us bound this am.

Oct. 22, 1942. New RAF chaps tied up. No wonder they haven't much to say.

Imagine 300 fellows washing clothes around two taps, and the inevitable confusion. Still, it was good to be free for nine whole hours.

Oct. 26, 1942. Mick and several others are put in chains.

Nov. 7, 1942. Have been tied up during the day for one month. The food situation remains poor and we are threatened with a diet of bread and water.

Nov. 10, 1942. The mail ban has been lifted. The tying up has finished and, instead, we are handcuffed with strong metal chains.

Nov. 20, 1942. All of us are now incapacitated with chains in lieu of cord.

Nov. 21, 1942. We are given a half day free of chains to clean our barracks etc. Generous Huns! Heavy snow.

Nov. 22, 1942. Terribly cold bathing in city water before early morning chains.

Nov. 24, 1942. The winter is here with a vengeance. Every day we wait outside for a couple of hours or so to be chained.

Nov. 27, 1942. Chains, chains, and still more chains.

We were kept in chains (handcuffed) for many months, not weeks. First it was with Red Cross string (rough cord) then poor quality "cuffs" which we learned to unlock though to be caught without them involved punishment. These "cuffs" were withdrawn and more sophisticated ones substituted which we soon learned how to unlock. We had the cuffs removed by the guards before "lights out" and were chained again at early morning roll call.

It was most difficult cleaning oneself wearing chains following defecation and most of us took a chance and unlocked one wrist. This was suspected by the guards who would, at times, rush in shouting and knocking us about whilst we were in a sitting position with our trousers down! Now I can see the funny side of it, but, at the time, it was far from amusing!

On December 8, 1942, the Swiss Government intervened with an appeal to the British, Canadian and German governments and suggested a date upon which the shackles should be removed.

Sept. 4, 1943. Trouble with Canadian NCOs and Australian airmen over manacles. No chains for us today! It appears we are losing them to Canadians and Army NCOs. We've had them long enough, its true, but I don't wish anyone else to go through the same ordeal as ourselves.

Nov. 23, 1943. Chains officially removed from the Dieppe chaps this morning and they are to be "allowed" (compelled) to "arbiet" (work) for the Fuhrer. The NCOs have been asked to volunteer!

Eric Herwin

It appears, from official records, that during the Dieppe raid the British issued an order that the hands of German prisoners were to be tied to prevent them destroying their papers. After the raid the Germans found and freed several German prisoners who had been bound and left behind. The tying of prisoners was repeated during a minor raid on Sark on October 3, some two months after the Dieppe raid.
As a reprisal the Germans shackled 1,373 British Commonwealth prisoners. On October 10 the Allies carried out the British Government's threat and shackled the same number of prisoners, most of them in Canada.

The Germans' response was to manacle three times the number of prisoners.
After the Swiss Government's intervention on December 8, the British and Canadian Governments freed all German prisoners from shackles on December 12. The Germans, however, continued the practice for some months before it was officially ceased on November 23, 1943, the date and event accurately recorded by Eric Herwin in his diary.

Atrocity

Not every prisoner taken by the enemy survived capture, or even got as far as a POW camp, as this gruesome incident in 1964 in Borneo demonstrates.

One Sunday we were due a visit from the Padre to conduct a church service at our outpost half a mile from the Indonesian border. Not that we were particularly religious, but it broke up the monotony and we could hear news from other places.

When the Padre, who was coming by helicopter, was over an hour late, fears grew for his safety. We sent out a patrol, going in the direction in which they had last heard from him and where he would be expected.

A few miles from us was a mountain range that was covered in dense jungle. Just over the mountain ridge we came across the wrecked helicopter. There was no sign of anyone, but the tracks showed us that several people had come to the crash site and that the two men from the helicopter had been dragged with them.

We followed the tracks for several hours and then came to a clearing.

The two had been tied to trees. The pilot had been tortured and castrated and his penis sewn in his mouth. The Padre suffered the same fate.

We were incensed and wanted to wreak revenge. But some of us had to get back with the bodies and the remainder went after the murderers. Unfortunately, they had a big start on us and we lost them over the border.

Ian Read

A living Hell

The evacuation of more than 300,000 troops from the beaches of Dunkirk during nine days in June 1940 tends to eclipse the fate of some 40,000 men who were left behind. Part of that group was the 51st Highland Division which was isolated at St. Valéry-en-Caux, more than 200 miles to the south-west of Dunkirk. They may have been tantalisingly close to the sea, but there was to be no rescue for those troops. On June 12, 1940, just a week after the Dunkirk evacuation had been completed, the besieged Division had to surrender following a heroic resistance.

I was serving with the RASC (Royal Army Service Corps) as part of the 51st Highland Division when it was captured by the Germans on June 10-12, 1940 at St. Valery.

I don't want to dwell on the following three months because the march to Germany was a living hell with hardly any food or water and we got weaker every day. The last part of our journey was by barge through Holland and Germany.

Then we were packed into cattle trucks, given three slices of bread at the start of a three day and night trip to Poland, and that was all the food we had on the journey.

Three months of anguish. Frank Tayler was captured at St. Valery in June 1940, but the official note to say he was a POW did not reach his family until three months later, such was the confusion after Dunkirk.

Men did the act of nature where they sat since we were packed in 48 to a truck and there was no room to move at all. I was lucky to have a position on the inside wall so I could lean on that and, as we did not have anything to drink, I was not troubled by not being able to get to the toilet.

When we reached the town of Thorn we were so weak that it was almost impossible to get to one's feet. After much effort and rifle bashing by the guards we managed to stumble about a mile to the Balloon Hanger which was to be our home for the next few weeks. It was there that we were given numbers. Mine was 1604. Our hair was shorn and it was discovered that we were lousy.

Rations were a litre of water-like soup and three slices of bread per day. There were three roll calls a day and these could take two to three hours. Standing in the hot sun in our weak state took a heavy toll and some of the men just could not survive that hardship and many passed away because of it.

In August 1940 we were moved to Fort 15. This was an underground fort and conditions improved there. But I was soon to lose my mate, Bert Rattery. We had been together since capture. I was now on my own. I managed to get on the spud peeling team and this kept me busy and earned an extra soup ration. That was a real bonus.

Then in September (1940) we were moved again, to Fort 17. A barber shaved us with cold water and I caught barber's rash after a few weeks. I had grown a beard and then I came out in boils. There wasn't any treatment and the pain was awful. One day, on roll call, the largest on the back of my neck burst and all the goo ran on to my shirt. I was now at my lowest and felt very ill.

Then on October 4 (1940) along with 300 others we were put on a train again and ended up at a wayside station called Gatowitz. Here a brand new camp had been built in the middle of a pine forest. My first thought was, could the smell of pines improve my health?

This camp had four blocks, each block had four rooms with 35-40 men per room, in bunk beds. I had a top bunk and my own space. What heaven!

One of the lads was concerned about my condition and one produced a razor with a new blade and said the first thing was to get rid of my beard. Blades were like gold dust at this time so it was a wonderful gesture to use one on me. After the operation I felt a lot better and then they set to work on my boils. One was on the back of my hand. It was murder as it was squeezed out, but it was worth it.

Rations were still five men to a German Army loaf and a litre of thin soup a day. Then, in November, the cold set in and we did not do much. During the cold winter days about the only work we did was to unload thousands of railway sleepers from trucks parked in the sidings at the small station. It was heavy work and each one had to be taken about half a mile to be stacked in neat piles. There were two men to a sleeper. Those trucks came in about twice a week and we wondered to what purpose they were going to be used in such an isolated spot.

We used to see the troop trains going eastwards and thought that one day they would be used against Russia. The other work we did was collecting wood for the camp which was cold and difficult in the deep snow.

In March (1941) a Red Cross food parcel arrived, one between 20 men. What a treat it was to have a small taste of real food: cream crackers, cheese and choc. Those parcels came from the Canadian Red Cross and were wonderful. Soon my strength began to come back and I was feeling fitter all the time. As we became more healthy the dreaded lice began to leave and soon they went altogether.

In May the snow melted and we were sent out to clear the forest and to make a start on big job roads, railways, and the other things the Germans had got planned . We were not looking forward to whatever it was.

Frank Tayler was moved to another camp on July 12, 1941, where prisoners were put to work on a new road. Conditions and food were better. Then he was sent to Stalag XXb. Marienburg.

Up to now our lives had been organised in the camp by British NCOs. But on arrival at Marienburg these were all taken away to spend their time in non-working camps. Now we were on our own with very little German to understand or speak.

It was a huge camp, each hut holding about 100 men.

We had to register again and our photos, which were taken at Thorn in August, 1940, were shown to us and I did not recognise myself! What a wreck I looked.

We found out we had been sent here to work in a sugar beet factory working 12 hours a day. A few of us went missing while these working parties were being made up. When we were found they had got the workers that were required for this job.

Next morning I was detailed, with nine others, to work on a farm. I was pleased because there is always food on a farm. So began a new life with comrades that I was to live with for the next three and a half years. No one could have had better mates and, in all, the bad times and the good, there were never any rows and we all looked after each other. Even when all ten of us had to live in one small room there was never any trouble. We always laughed at our trouble and enjoyed each other's company. At the end of the day each would tell about the things he had done and many a good tale was told.

Frank Tayler

Repatriation.

Under the terms of the Geneva Convention on the treatment of prisoners of war, which both Germany and Britain had ratified, severely wounded and sick prisoners who were unfit for active service and other protected personnel such as medical staff and padres, surplus to requirements in the prison camps and hospitals, were to be exchanged without regard to rank or numbers.

Those who qualified and had been certified as such by an international medical commission were termed "Grand Blessé" *(seriously injured).*

In November 1940 I was one of a number who had been wounded in May and June who were still in the German-controlled Belgian Military Hospital at Ghent. One of our number had been a POW in the 1914-18 war and knew all about prisoner exchanges. So, when the Germans ordered a list to be made of all who could stand a 36-hour rail journey in ordinary compartments, we immediately thought of Switzerland or Sweden and everyone who could get out of bed put down their names.

On November 10 the "volunteers" were marched to the station. The remainder were taken by ambulance or lorry. The train, which had continental wooden seated coaches as well as Birmingham-made ambulance coaches, presumably left by the BEF, was waiting.

After picking up more patients at Malines we proceeded up the Rhine valley reaching Frankfurt in an air raid. A few miles further south at Dieburg we left the train, the lucky ones by lorry, and the "volunteers" on foot. Many of the latter group had a real struggle and had to dump the pathetic bundles of clothes etc. which kind Belgians and French had given them.

In January 1941 an International Medical Commission, which was going round the hospitals and camps, arrived.

No one knew how bad one had to be to qualify. This led to some hilarious episodes with men endeavouring to maximise their disability. It appeared, however, that the Commission members were generally sympathetic. They departed and weeks and months passed. Nothing was heard of repatriation until September when all those who had passed were assembled from their various hospitals and camps and moved across France to Rouen.

We were told that there was to be a temporary armistice and a cross-channel exchange. There were, at that time, well over 1,000 British "Grand Blessé", but not more than 100 Germans. The latter were already on board a British hospital ship in Newhaven harbour.

We did not, of course, know of this but about 100 of us were segregated from the rest, given the most thorough search we had had so far, and moved to another building. After further delay and many rumours we were taken by lorry to the railway station where a Swiss ambulance train was waiting with blind and other seriously wounded on board. The train started off and, in our carriage, we were discussing where we were going - Le Havre, Dieppe, Frecamp - when a Swiss orderly came into the coach. We asked him.

He asked: "Don't you know?"

We said: "No."

He said: "You are going back to Germany! The exchange is off!"

I learned later, when serving in the War Office, that Hitler had said that they would count the number of Germans off the boat and put the same number of British on, demanding civilian internees or unwounded to equalise the number. Churchill refused to bargain. This was undoubtedly a correct decision, but one which caused us great distress. It would have been even worse had we known that we had another two years of captivity in front of us.

The ambulance train took us back to the British-staffed hospital in central Germany, but the unfortunates who we left in Rouen were in due course moved to Poland where they had to endure the very bitter winter of 1941-42.

I was fortunate as the surgeon who had looked after me in Dieburg told me that I required a further operation. He had the facilities to do it with a first class colleague who would assist. To do it now would save hospitalisation when I got home. The operation was successful and, on April 1, 1942, I was moved to a POW camp.

After two more moves and a week in a German Military hospital to have my appendix removed, the only occasion since the first week when I was treated by a German, I was repatriated via Sweden in October 1943.

I had been told by a friendly German that the Germans would abide by the terms of the Geneva Convention, but that there would be technical hitches until there were as many German Grand Blessé in British hands as there were British in German hands. So it proved. For, when Tunisia fell and hospitals in North Africa were overrun it was only a matter of weeks before the first exchange took place.

Denis Dodd

Chapter 9

The Cookhouse Door

*Bad men live that they may eat and drink, whereas
good men eat and drink that they may live.* SOCRATES

Life-line food parcels

My first real POW camp (September 1942) was at a place called Benevento, just a few miles north of Naples. Here I was brought down to earth to experience a rather more primitive existence. There were lines of tents, with duckboards on which to sleep, extremely primitive sanitation, and meagre rations.

We did have an issue of Red Cross food parcels, one between seven men which created something of a problem.

One group, I remember, decided to divide each item into seven parts so that each member received his portion there and then. One seventh of a tin of spam, of a tin of jam, of a tin of butter etc., right through each item.

What was most unusual was when one member of the group had his seventh of each item placed in his dixie, all together, and proceeded to eat the lot with a spoon.

When it came to dividing any food between any group the item in questions would be cut up into equal parts and then each part given a number and hidden behind the back of one of the group. Each member in turn would then call out a number and receive the correspondingly numbered portion. In this way no one could deliberately take a larger share than anyone else. One of the first things I noticed on entering the camp was a POW handcuffed and fastened by the wrists to the perimeter wire. Apparently he had been caught stealing another POW's item of food and was thus dealt with by the senior NCO in the compound as a warning to others.

Fred Frost, who had been captured at Tobruk in June 1942 was moved from camp to camp the length of Italy and, in January 1943, was moved to a well-established camp at Chiavari near Genoa.

The food was pretty well the same every day, a bread roll and sometimes a small piece of cheese or salami sausage mid-morning and a dixie of macaroni with some sort of tomato puree in the evening.

Fortunately we received a Red Cross food parcel fairly regularly, on average I would say it was one between two per week. They contained things like a tin of meat loaf, a tin of jam, and one of butter, biscuits, a packet of tea or coffee, a bar of chocolate, and a small tin of dried egg flakes.

These parcels had all been packed in various locations in the UK and stamped on the cardboard containers was the place of origin. I remember Bermondsey, Northampton, Cardiff etc, each of them having a slightly different combination of items.

Sometimes the Germans released official photographs of happy and relaxed British POWs for propaganda purposes. This one, of prisoners playing football, was at Camp E719, in Silesia, where Fred Frost was held.

I think probably the favourite among us were the Canadian food parcels. They contained a fair sized tin of KLIM (milk spelt backwards of course) this was powdered milk, a packet of large round biscuits and a packet of dried raisins. With these three items it was possible to make a very tasty sort of bread pudding.

Small individual groups of POWs made their own "blowers" on which to do any cooking whenever ingredients became available. The "blowers" were made by hammering out flat empty tins into sheets eight or nine inches square, and using them to construct a fan with a duct leading to a fire box. A wheel made from the circular ends of the tins was attached by a string belt to the fan, so that when it was turned at high speed the draught caused quite a lot of heat to be generated from the fire. Fuel was something of a problem. Gradually bed boards disappeared so that the occupants of the upper bunks were in grave danger of falling through on the occupants below.

After an issue of Red Cross parcels a bit of trading went on with the guards. A bar of soap, a packet of tea, or a bar of chocolate went for a loaf of bread or a dozen fresh eggs. During the night one was likely to be awakened by a "clucking" noise close by one's bed. In the darkness it was just possible to make out a guard holding a cardboard box of eggs, offering them for a bar of soap or something.

The other way was to meet a guard patrolling outside the wire out of sight of the sentry towers and do a deal there. A packet of tea for instance would be thrown up over the wire and back would come a loaf of bread. Each side regarded the other with suspicion so that the transaction was only carried out if both items were thrown simultaneously.

A POW demonstrates a 'blower', a fan improvised from empty tins, together with a duct, which led to the cooking firebox. It caused more heat to be generated. A wheel, made from the circular ends of tins, was attached by a string belt to the fan.

It was considered a good idea to use the contents of the tea packet first, dry the leaves again, return them to the packet and seal it up neatly before doing the deal. That soon put a stop to that operation when the guards found that their tea did not come up to expectation.

Fred Frost

Dangerous dishes

I reported to the kitchen and was put on day shift and on all the main dishes.

You work your seniority by what you do in the kitchen. A new boy, just out of training, would be on veg. preparation, and the one above him would be responsible for cooking it, along with the new boy. More senior persons would go on salad and pies in the larder department, followed by the pastry department. After pastry, and just before the main meats, comes the butcher's shop where all the meat is cut and dissected for all the three Messes.

The Officers' Mess usually got the better cuts of meat, the Sergeants' Mess the next best, the Other Ranks' Mess getting the leftovers. But that did not necessarily mean that the ORs ate any less well than the Officers.

The definition of the chef is - anyone can be a cook and make something with all the ingredients, but a chef can make something from nothing.

There was a contingent of Australians stopping with us (in Terendack Camp, Malacca), and feeding in our Mess. They were on R&R from Vietnam. As their rations were larger than ours they were able to have steak for breakfast as well as the traditional English greasy Joe's breakfast. This did nothing for the morale of our troops and they whinged every breakfast time.

The cry was: "Why can't we have steak?"

We retorted that they were only cannon fodder and not worth the price of a steak! This had the effect of shutting them up, either because they couldn't think of a decent retort, or coming to near blows.

Sometimes it's more dangerous being a cook than being in the SAS!

Ian Read

Feeding 'the enemy'

The poverty hit you the moment you drove across the border from Kuwait into Southern Iraq. The villages and homes were run down and shabby, there was no livestock, and the people appeared to be living close to starvation level after years under Saddam's regime.

As we drove into one village near Safwan the inhabitants fled indoors at the sight of an enemy vehicle, though the children were less inhibited. We stopped the Land Rover in the centre and placed one or two tins of compo on doorsteps, keeping our delivery girl covered in case of an ambush. It didn't take many minutes for emaciated-looking children to emerge and surround our vehicle pleading for more tins of food.

We emptied the box of compo rations and they went off with wide smiles clutching tins of pork products, forgetting they were Muslims.

The Americans were quick to set up feeding points close to the border for the Iraqi civilians and they also provided rudimentary medical treatment where necessary.

At another spot, we watched Iraqi soldiers changing from uniform into their loose-fitting civilian robes before coming across the border to surrender, perhaps to join the queue for food.

Aubrey Chalmers

Whistle stop eating

Living conditions were intolerable (Chong-Song POW Camp, North Korea, 1951). The camp was hopelessly overcrowded. We lay on the floor, ten men to a small room, head to foot with less than a square yard to each man. The roof leaked and the only contribution made by the Chinese was a blanket between two men.

The daily calorie intake was negligible - rough maize twice a day was the norm when we first arrived. Then we got a sandy millet which was worse. Rice we had every ten or fourteen days - it was indeed a luxury.

The Chinese at first adopted a whistle stop type of feeding that went something like this:

We would line up with our tins, bowls or hats, or whatever container we had grabbed on our way north. (The Chinese had relieved each man on capture of all

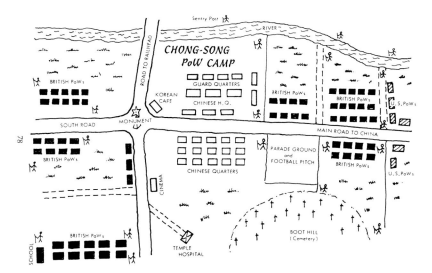

Plan of the POW camp in Korea.

items of equipment such as small packs, mess tins, and washing and shaving gear). We would then sit around with our food until everyone was served - a great ordeal for starving men.

Then the whistle was blown and everyone started eating, most with their hands. Those that finished their first helping rushed back for more, that is, if there was anything left. The Phillipinos being rice-eaters always made it to the fore.

When the allotted time was up the Chinese guard blew the whistle again and everyone had to stop. Woe-betide the man who tried to eat later. It was very rough justice on sick men who had difficulty in getting the coarse food down, but, I am glad to say, this practice wasn't to last for long.

As the weeks went by the food did not improve and everyone was very thin. Soon we began to suffer from a type of scabies. Malnutrition caused our tongues and mouths to become red and raw. Dysentery abounded and became the norm. We also began to suffer from what was known as "bone pains". These were pains mostly in the thigh bones and legs which occurred at night or when resting.

The news that we were to be released came one morning in late July (1953).

Almost immediately extra food appeared and, for the next few weeks, we were fed three times a day with fresh meat. Rice and bread was also available in large quantities. Sweets and cigarettes were also issued en masse as well as soaps and toothpaste. We all began to put on weight and, by the time the International Red Cross visited the camp, we all looked a lot healthier.

Henry O'Kane

Chinese slug soup

On arrival at Sian, the old capital of China, (in June 1945) we went first to the Travel Service Hotel, in which General Ho's influence got us rooms. We were then given an immense dinner, starting with sea slug soup (I fortunately didn't know what they were until they were too far gone to worry me). Mrs Ho was a very charming lady, daughter of a well known divine. She understood English but did not speak it.

After about 20 dishes we staggered into rickshaws - pneumatic tyres per favour of the Japs - and were wheeled away to the hotel where we had cold baths and relapsed on to the bed.

English breakfast, three eggs, dry toast, cup of coffee (275$) and off in rickshaws to Mr Ho's.

We then went to the Baptist Mission compound to rent a Baptist house and we took over one of the mission houses. General Ho and Mrs Ho occupied the end room and Adrian and I had a room each. There was a sitting room and a small dining room.

The kitchen and cook's quarters were by the side and there was a nice patio with a shrubbery. Mrs Ho organised the meals. We ate twice a day. Breakfast was eggs and bread and anything we could find to put on it. The main meal, about 2 pm, usually was of four Chinese dishes, egg, shredded meat and vegetables, and chicken.

Mr Ho had spent 700,000$ on us purely in feasts to give us face and start us off on the right foot. To cap it General Wang, second in command to Marshal Hu Zung Nan, did the unprecedented and gave us lunch... what a lunch. He was pretty unapproachable by Europeans, especially with our lowly ranks. The fish alone cost 20,000$.

John Stanfield

Stalag V111b, Silesia

Dec. 18, '42. Jack and I went for early 'tea' and were out of bed at 5.30 am. We saw about two dozen of our guards sampling our tea before we took possession of the keeble. The bastards must wangle about 50% of our rations and our own countrymen are equally to blame.

It was customary for us to have a keeble of German mint tea from the cookhouse in the early morning. It was used for shaving during the winter and as a beverage both summer and winter when drinking water was unavailable.

In 1942 and early 1943 we, very occasionally, had *real* tea made from Red Cross tea which arrived in camp in the customary three-ply boxes of about one cubic yard. We put a stop to this practice because the British cookhouse staff stole so much of the dry tea and sold it on their own black market. From then on it was distributed to compounds and barracks dry, for us to make our own tea instead of it being made in the cookhouse.

Our mid-day soup was brought into the barrack in a dustbin-like container called a keeble. It was not unknown for some of the duty carriers to guzzle some of it on passage from the cookhouse to barrack. We all queued for the soup, the same position every day, but every day you moved up one place. This was to ensure that everyone had his share in getting thin or less thin soup.

Those first in the queue had thin but hot soup. Those at the end had the thickest. Occasionally the soup was short in quantity and then one or more men would get none. Similarly, there would occasionally be one or two left over rations, in which case there was a roster so that every man had his fair share.

When the last of the soup was distributed a cry would go up "Keeble Scrapers!" This was the sign for the uninhibited to rush to the keeble and scrape (often with their hands and fingers) for the fragments of soup left on the inside of the keeble.

We had one chap, an airgunner, who invariably got to the keeble first. He was paranoid over it, and admitted he could not control his action as he feared he was slowly dying of starvation. I think all of us would have liked to be keeble scrapers, but our feelings of shame prevented us from doing so.

It was always those prisoners who kept tight control of their life style who managed to survive difficult situations.

The cookhouse at V111b. was staffed by a British sergeant (Army) and about 10 junior ranks under the overall supervision of a German feldwebel *(sergeant)*.

The job attracted the more unreliable elements within the camp and they creamed off the best of the food and either sold it or gave it to fellow ne'er-do-wells. Potatoes, swedes, turnips and cabbage were never washed properly, if washed at all, and rotting vegetables would not be removed before cooking in the huge cauldrons.

I remember an occasion when our soup keeble contained a horse's head complete with hair, also a day when we discovered a cooked mouse and on another occasion a cooked kitten.

The shock of finding a horse's head in the soup no doubt made Eric Herwin fail to appreciate the irony of the situation. The badge of 35 Squadron, to which he belonged, was a winged horse's head. The Motto: "We act with one accord."

Jan. 24, '43. Issue of 'honey' and margarine.

The German issue of margarine, so-called honey and jam, fish, cheese, and sausage, was minuscule. It was, nevertheless, a highlight of our existence because, for most of the time, we were denied Red Cross food and were existing on one pint of thin cabbage or potato soup, two slices of black bread and half a pint of mint tea each day. If one was lucky there would be a few grease spots (and once a horse's head) in the soup.

But it was far from a sustaining diet. In fact, it was barely sufficient to maintain sedentary life let alone an active one. Food was all important to us and, looking back, I can understand why some of us behaved like hungry pigs at a trough!

May 30, '43. None of the Hun food, apart from the bread and potatoes, has been edible for some weeks. Intermittent issues of Red Cross food staves off starvation. The potato ration of three-quarters of a pound is meant to be a daily issue but is not often issued. They are usually well boiled but are not sorted beforehand. Consequently the ration includes straw, stones, soil and rotten tubers. They would not be given to pigs at home because of the stones and the rots.

Sept. 20, '43. My tummy has shrunk so much that I never feel hungry these days. In fact, I'm giving almost all my bread away.

Sept. 17, '44. Terrific rushings around today - Huns in a great panic - they say that from now on any tins of Red Cross food issued to us will be stabbed beforehand. We are already having to throw away fish and other food which becomes contaminated after a few hours.

It was frustrating to stand in line waiting for a precious Red Cross parcel and to see and hear each tin being holed with a guard's bayonet. This was to render it less suitable for use when trying to escape. Following unacceptable behaviour by us the enemy would occasionally open up the tins and food packages and tip the contents - meat, milk, sugar, tea, chocolate etc., into the cardboard box before handing it to us. It was like eating thick pig swill.

Nov. 22, '44. The food situation is becoming ever more critical.

Nov. 24, '44. Huns have commenced bayonetting chaps for pinching spuds from the wagons.

We were all undernourished and this provided the right climate for thieving. The answer was more food provided by the Germans but we had no priority - only the armed forces and civilian workers were reasonably well provided for. Theft of bread, potatoes and swede or cabbage soup, meant that there was less for those not involved with racketeering.

Nov. 26, '44. A chap was shot through the foot trying to steal coal whilst another was badly bashed yesterday whilst trying to get a few spuds. He was covered in bayonet weals.

Thieving was rife amongst POWs and even close associates occasionally stole from their mates. The temptation to steal food and clothing when conditions were bad was overwhelming to some. Clothing and other personal possessions would be lifted and traded on the camp black market. One of our syndicate members even stole on a regular basis some of our tiny ration of black bread when, sometimes for months on end, we were denied Red Cross food parcels. I didn't accuse him but he knew that I knew he was guilty and had betrayed our confidence.

There were occasions when caught in the act of theft the person concerned was executed! Others were ostracised and some of those committed suicide.

I believe the recommended daily calories intake for a working adult is in the region of 2,500. As a prisoner I was often without food and water, but our captors did not agree that a daily intake of 800 calories for POWs, not in heavy paid employment, was adequate. Give the Germans their due, they applied the same criteria to their own nationals.

When one is really hungry all sensations, including the feeling of pain or fear of death, are secondary to the animal instinct to eat. It's a sad state when a helping of lukewarm liquid in a tin makes the unfed body tremble in anticipation or when a person risks death by shooting just to grab a swede from a clamp in the field. But that is how it was.

Eric Herwin

The Gestapo march out empty handed after an abortive search of the camp. A cheeky POW took a picture of them with a camera they had failed to find.

Chapter 10

Letters from Home

...will you please say hello to the folks that I know,
Tell 'em I won't be long,
Ross Parker & Hughie Charles, 1939 - We'll Meet Again

Her lips had sealed the envelope

Frank Tayler was captured with the 51st Highland Division at St. Valery on June 10, 1940. He survived appalling conditions on the route across Europe before being held at a POW camp at Gullowitz, Poland, in October 1940 - July 1945.

Up to now survival had been the only thought but now Lil and home became an obsession and were always in my thoughts. Did Lil know my fate? What was she doing? How I longed for night to come so that sleep would relieve me of the pain.

In November (1940) the cold set in and it was about this time that I received my first letter from Lil. Wonderful! Wonderful to hold it in my hands. My loved one's own writing. Her lips had sealed the envelope. I was in heaven.

Her newsy letters were full of the things I had been longing to hear. I had about 14 in a week and became known in the camp as the man who got all the mail. Every one in the hut wanted to read my letters. From now on mail was fairly regular and I always had more than anyone.

In February (1941) I received a parcel from Lil. It was wonderful! She had put in precious things, socks, short books, razor blades, soap, needles and thread, and many other things. During the next four years she sent me regular parcels. The contents kept me warm and clean and helped my well-being. She must have sacrificed a lot to send me these parcels.

Then in March a Red Cross food parcel arrived - one between 20 men. What a treat it was to have a small taste of real food. Cream crackers, cheese and choc. Those parcels came from Canada Red Cross and were wonderful.

Frank E W Tayler

The mail has been destroyed

Our only sources of news were the three months old *Daily Workers* from London or old copies lf the *Shanghai News*.

We wrote regular letters home but received only a few letters in return. We were to learn later that very few ever got home. A prisoner received perhaps one letter in three months. I didn't receive more than six in all the time I was there. Other than letters no other mail was ever received by UN POWs in North Korea.

Items such as newspapers, magazines, books and comfort parcels which were posted to us regularly we were never allowed to have by the Chinese. In answer to the many complaints about the lack of mail our captors always used the same excuse - the mail had been destroyed by American bombing.

Henry O'Kane

God Bless Andrea

Late in August 1944, during a lull in the Battle of Normandy, we found ourselves in a French village about five miles inland from Dieppe. A message came through that a French lady wished to speak to a British officer and, as my jeep was available, I was detailed to collect our Intelligence Officer and take him to the lady's home.

After a glass of Calvados she explained that two years before, during August 1942, after the disastrous raid on Dieppe (carried out mainly by Canadians) a French-speaking Canadian officer was taken prisoner by the Germans, but had managed to escape and, in the confusion, came to her door and asked for shelter.

Although she knew the enormous risk she was taking, she agreed to take him in. She explained that had she been discovered she would have been on her way quickly to Ravensbrück Concentration Camp. When things quietened down she contacted the French underground for help. She was told he would be collected in due course; she understood that he would be moved from place to place and finally over the Pyrenees to Spain, a neutral country.

Before he left, however, he wrote some letters and these were buried in the orchard.

He asked that when the liberation came that she would hand the letters to the liberators.

We went out into the orchard and she pointed to the spot whey they lay buried. I was ordered to get the shovel from the jeep and start digging. About two feet down I came to a tin. In it were three letters, one addressed to his CO, one to his mother, and one to his fiancée. I assume that these letters explained what had happened to him if he did not survive and record the help he had received from this lady.

The Intelligence Officer took charge of the letters and I assume that they were posted to their rightful owners.

Every night the BBC would broadcast to occupied Europe with personal messages. These always commenced with the Morse letter V (**...** -).

It had been agreed that should the Canadian be fortunate enough to get back to the UK he would endeavour to arrange for a message to be sent to her and that it should read "GOD BLESS ANDREA".

Sure enough, about a month later, the message was transmitted. She told us how delighted she was and felt that she had done her bit for the war effort.

Ironically her son, who was in the French Navy, was killed by the British when they opened fire and sank a number of French ships at Oran, on the North African coast, in 1940. At the time it was feared that these ships were about to join the German Navy so no chances were taken.

She did not blame the British for the tragedy which cost her son ANDREA his life. I often wondered if the Canadian officer survived the subsequent D-Day landings in 1944 and looked up this very brave and courageous lady.

Clive Pitt

The dreaded telegram

Eric Herwin and Iris were married in November 1941. Iris continued living at home at Saltash and working in Plymouth, writing every day to her husband who was serving with the RAF. At the end of July 1942 she made a hazardous train journey, interrupted by bombing, to visit him at Linton on Ouse, near York. The arrangements for the week-end became a disaster and, after waiting for two hours outside the camp gates, Iris managed to snatch a four hour reunion with her husband before travelling back to Plymouth.

I was always so very thankful I made that journey as it was the last time we were together for two years and eight months. I was expecting a telegram at home any time to say he was coming on leave. When it arrived and I opened it, it was to say he was missing.

That was a dreadful time but I was so very very fortunate.

Iris Herwin

If only Iris knew

Aug. 18, '42. I have written my first letter home.

Aug. 22, '42. I think to myself, if only Iris knew that I am safe and well-treated and in good health, how happy she would be and how much less troubled her mind.

Aug. 23, '42. I have written and posted my second letter home. Have also written two postcards.

Aug. 24, '42. I trust Iris has received news of me by now.

Aug. 25 '42. Wrote my third PC to Iris. A glorious full moon last night -

my thoughts are with my sweetheart and I can't help feeling how very happy we'd be in each other's arms at our gate in *our* lane.

Eric Herwin

I went crazy with joy

I think he bribed a German guard and I had a post card from him in three weeks to say he was safe but a POW and that all his crew were with him.

The postman, knowing I was at work, saw what it was and brought it to me at my office instead of to the home address. I think I went mildly crazy with joy. I immediately sent telegrams to the NOK of all the crew saying I had heard from Eric and that all the crew were with him and safe. None of the other NOK heard anything, apart from what I told them, in months and it was certainly the quickest communication I ever had while he was a POW.

Although I wrote immediately it was a very long time before Eric started getting letters from me.

Iris Herwin

As though she was talking to me

October 22, '42. A red letter day. A day of indescribable joy. Three lovely letters from my own darling sweetheart. The wonder of knowing that she and all my loved ones are safe and well. The wonder of hearing once again that Iris loves me. The two photographs are perfect. I am the envy of many. How I'd love to write pages and pages in return. Her letters seemed just right as though she was talking to me Everyone must have been greatly troubled when I was reported missing and news of my survival a great relief.

Oct. 23, '42. A horribly wet day. My heart is warm though, warmed with the letters of my loved one. I derive much comfort re-reading yesterday's letters and studying two happy snapshots. What a glorious honeymoon.

Eric Herwin

Every single word was precious

The permitted allowance was originally two post cards and two letters all on issued forms per calendar month. Eric often "bought" more with cigarettes etc. from POWs who didn't bother to write or, in some cases, had no one to write to.

Every single word was precious, read and re-read, and always loving and cheerful. Ours was a very special relationship.

Letters were frequently censored, blacked out so heavily that it was sometimes virtually impossible to make sense of them. It was only when I read his diaries that I even guessed the horrors that went on.

About once a year there would be a photograph - propaganda - with clothing issued and taken back again to make them look well cared for.

Clothing parcels could be sent every few months, up to 9 lbs. in weight. Forms were sent to NOK and we were informed of what could and could not be included. All our sweet rations went and many of our friends gave me theirs as chocolate could be included and, if the parcel was under weight, the Red Cross would include extra chocolate to make up the weight.

It was also possible, periodically, to sent money to the Imperial Tobacco Company for them to send a parcel. Cigarettes were used as currency. I sent all I could. Much never arrived. Book parcels, packed and despatched by publishers, could be ordered and paid for.

Our old postman who, I am sure, must have worked on well beyond retiring age, would often be walking back to the Post Office at lunch time and would always be so pleased to tell me if there was a letter for me. If it was a post card he would quite openly tell me he had read it and that Eric was OK. I suspect he passed the information around as I would often get people saying, "I gather you have heard from Eric and he is OK",

I worked out a system for numbering my letters by increasing the number of the house on my address each time I wrote. I mentioned to Eric a couple of times to note the "change of address". He quickly caught on so he knew how many letters were missing.

There was no accounting for the order in which they arrived, in either direction. Sometimes they would be only five weeks old and, on other occasions, two or three months.

I constantly wrote to the overseas NOK, as all their mail came first to England from POWs and then it was sent on to their own countries. Eric realised the situation and would give me what news he had and I would pass it on by air mail. There was a means by which even civilian letters by air mail were reduced by copying to microscopic size and then enlarged again at the other end so that they were normal size again when delivered. Everything, of course, was censored.

Sometimes I wrote to other POWs whom I had never met, simply because Eric would tell me they rarely, if ever, received letters. One or two very sick POWs who were repatriated wrote to me on their return to England and I had some news that way. Eric had asked them to do that.

During the last six months of the war mail dried up altogether. There were newspaper reports, which were very sketchy, saying that POW camps in Poland had been overrun by the Russians. We really had no idea what had happened.

Iris Herwin

Stalag V111b. Silesia.

Dec. 23, 1942. Four wonderful letters from my darling and a birthday card and the two photographs from my wallet. How very lovely to have them. This is my Christmas present - in the circumstances the loveliest present I can receive. I've read and re-read the letters four times already. They set the old heart throbbing madly!

Sept. 22, 1943. Received a lovely letter today from my darling. I'm floating on air! Often wonder what sort of fellow I'd be - what sort of life I would lead if it wasn't for her wonderful love for me.

Nov. 3, 1943. Seven lovely letters from my Iris - written June, July and August. Included were three snapshots, one of which (Iris alongside bicycle) is exceptionally good.

Nov. 25, 1943. Four lovely letters from my sweetheart. Have had to destroy a lot of letters today. It's something I hate doing here especially as they are so precious.

Nov. 26, 1943. Have had to destroy numerous letters from home again, but will have to do more. A hateful job.

Letters were highly prized, even at their end. They provided heat in our tiny stoves sufficient to heat a mug of water.

Dec. 21, 1943. Two chaps in this barrack have today had letters from their wives asking for immediate divorces - wives have met other fellows. One of the POWs allowed another to take his place on repatriation, and it is this "thankful and considerate bastard" who is now living with his wife.

If I remember correctly the official letter allowance was one letter or two postcards per month. Some prisoners wrote few, if any, letters home while I greatly exceeded my allowance, though it was against the German rules.

My supply of extra letters was mainly by courtesy of the Polish air crew and one Czech - half a dozen of whom occupied bunks beside me. They could not write home because their countries were occupied by the common enemy, hence I was sometimes offered their card issue.

For a host of reasons some chaps rarely received letters from home. Most of them put a brave face on this, but I know with some the hurt was accentuated by others receiving both letters and parcels.

I learned subsequently that senders were very strictly limited in what they could enclose in parcels which must not exceed 9 lbs in weight. Chocolate could be included and this was provided for me from the limited sweet ration of Iris, family and friends. The Red Cross would also enclose some chocolate if the parcel was left underweight.

Everything had to be listed and packed in a certain way and sent to the Red Cross for repacking, checking,and forwarding to the POWs. The official forms were sent to next of kin every three months to allow the parcels to be sent.

Eric Herwin

Last Letter Home

April 21, 1915.

Dear Mother and Father, sisters and brothers,

Just a few lines to let you know I am in the best of health and hope you are mother. I am sorry to have to tell you that I am to be shot tomorrow at 7 o'clock in the morning the 22nd April.

I hope you will take it in good part and not upset yourself. I shall die like a soldier, so goodbye mother, father, sisters and brothers, if any left.

Remember me to Mr Kendall and them who knew me. Mother I am very sorry nothing happened to me at Ypres. I should not have went away and then I might have stood a good chance of being still alive, but I think they are paying the debt at the full rate. I thought the most they would give me would be about ten years. It is worse than waiting to be hung.

I hope you got my letters which I sent you while waiting for my court martial. It seems that something told me I would be shot, so I think the time has come for me to die . . . I am only a common soldier and all civilians should know that I have fought for my country in hail, sleet and snow. To the trenches we have to go. All my comrades have been slaughtered which I think everyone should know.

When our Regiment was captured the colonel loudly strained: "Everyone for hiself." But on and on I fought and got clear of the German trenches. This is the punishment I get for getting clear of the Germans.

I have wrote my last letter to you all at home, so mother don't be angry with me because I have gone to rest, and pray for me, and I will pray for you.

Remember me to Mr Newbold and tell him about it . . . I have been silly to go away but if you knew how worried I was, and almost off my head. Think how we had been slaughtered at the beginning of the war . . . you think they would have a bit of pity for those who are living and dying for their country.

Good bye to all at home. Goodbye, Goodbye,

From your son, Albert.

Albert Troughton wrote his last letter home the night before he faced a firing squad on April 22, 1915.

This short piece of First World War writing, smuggled from the Ypres front by Army jailors to the writer's family, came to my attention in late 1998 through reading the script of a half-hour play *Rough Justice* written by a fellow writer from Coventry, Bob Ashmore. A copy of Albert's letter had been in the Ashmore family for many years. In prompted Bob to investigate the history and write his play.

Lt. General (later Field Marshal) Douglas Haig had confirmed the death sentence "as a deterrent to others". This was in spite of Albert having followed his own commanding officer's last order of "every man for himself" as nearly 300 comrades of the 1st Battalion Royal Welsh Fusiliers were being slaughtered all round him.

Albert fought his way clear of the Germans. He was then told, by an officer, that one of his three fighting brothers had been killed down the line. Albert wandered off in shock. Later arrested, he was returned to his unit where all who could have vouched for him were dead - or alive in the hands of the Germans.

Lower ranks in those days were not allowed representation at courts martial. Albert's fine record allowed him neither exemption from King's Regulations nor mention of his contribution to the war effort, save for his momentary lapse. These regulations were revised after the 1914-18 Great War "to end all wars."

Thus, the night of April 21, 1915, saw private Albert Troughton penning his Last Letter Home. It says much of him that his army jailors risked charges by smuggling the letter to his family in Foleshill, Coventry after his execution.

The soldier's death was reported in the *Coventry Graphic* as "killed in action." Many families, ashamed to discover their loved ones had been executed by firing squad, were happy to hide behind this fiction. But not the Troughton family. It is said that they kept their son's last letter home on the mantelpiece and would show it to visitors to prove that he had been treated unjustly. They were not ashamed to speak of what had happened.

Martyn Richards

10853 Pte. A. Troughton, aged 22, was one of two men who faced the firing squad on the morning of April 22, 1915. The other was 10958 Pte. Major Penn who was also accused of desertion. It was the fifth double execution to take place and, before the two men from the Royal Welsh Fusiliers were shot, there had been 27 previous executions following Courts Martial on the Western Front.

Field Post Card

This is the story of a soldier. He was not famous. He was not decorated for bravery. But his story represents every ordinary soldier who served his country.

His name was Joe and his war was the so-called "Great War", the "War to End All Wars" - the First World War.

When war was declared (August 4, 1914) Joe was on holiday in Oxford. His immediate reaction was to cut short his holiday, return home, and sign up. He had been born and raised in Nechells, Birmingham, It was natural therefore that he should join his local regiment, the Royal Warwicks. Having completed his basic training Joe was given leave and then left with the 9th Battalion for the Dardanelles.

During the campaign he distinguished himself as good soldier. At one stage his platoon was pinned down by sniper fire; the sniper had been responsible for the deaths of many British soldiers over a short period.

Joe and his mate were given the task of trying to locate and eliminate the sniper. By careful observation the two men established where he was concealed and, taking turns to fire to observe the effect, they set about the task of dislodging him. It was Joe's second shot that found the mark and the sniper was dead.

For their work the two soldiers were told by their platoon commander that he intended to recommend them for a decoration. However, the officer was killed shortly thereafter, before having the opportunity to complete his report. The official history of the Warwicks. shows that, at this time, the CSM commanded the Battalion for a short time as all the officers had been killed - so severely had the 9th been mauled.

For many months the only contact that the family had was the occasional brief letter. They believed that Joe was serving somewhere in a desert area but did not know exactly where.

The family of John Curry, from the Royal Warwickshire Regiment, identified him (circled) on an old WW1 film. At Christmas 1915 the only thing that the soldiers could exchange as a presents were clips of .303 ammunition which Pte. Curry's family kept for many years afterwards. Photograph courtesy of the Imperial War Museum, London.

Then, one day, towards the end of 1915, quite suddenly and without warning, he arrived home. To the family's concern he arrived still in desert kit, bloodstained and battered but unbowed.

It transpired that, just prior to withdrawal, the trench he was in was hit by shellfire and he had been buried alive for a few minutes. He stayed for a brief couple of hours before continuing to barracks having "given himself leave" while in transit! Two days later he was home again, fully re-kitted and officially on leave for four days.

Only too soon his leave was over and he was off again. This time he had volunteered for France. His next Christmas was spent in the trenches of the front line as a member of the 2nd Battalion. Like many other soldiers he had no possessions with him - nothing to give his best mate for Christmas. So they swapped clips of five rounds of .303 ammunition.

Once again, the family at home lost touch with him.

During July, 1916, Joe was wounded in the Battle of the Somme. His family learned of this when they received what was called a "field post card" from him. The pre-printed post card carried several options for the soldier to choose from, by deleting the ones that did not apply.

From the field hospital the soldier simply crossed out as required, addressed the front, and the card was sent to England. The message stated simply: "I have been wounded. I am doing well." The card was addressed in Joe's own hand.

Some days later a second card arrived. This time it said: "I've been wounded. I am being looked after."

But it was clear that it had not been addressed by Joe. Though the family did not know it, Joe was, in fact, dying. Soon afterwards came the official War Office notification that he had "died of wounds."

Months later Joe's mate (whose name, sadly, is now unknown) returned to England on leave and was able to visit the family and tell them the full story.

During the early hours of the morning the 2nd Battalion had been moved to the reserve trenches. On about the 14th July Joe was actually "resting" when an enemy artillery round came in, either as a deliberate long shot or by accident. The young soldier received the shrapnel wounds which were to end his life.

His friend gave Joe's mother the last and only memento he had of her son . . . the clip of rifle bullets that Joe had given him for Christmas The clip of five rounds lay on the kitchen fireplace, above an open fire, for the next 40-odd years.

Pte 2716 Joseph Curry, 9th, later the 2nd Battalion, the Royal Warwickshire Regiment, died of wounds on July 24, 1916. He lies in Heilly Station Military Cemetery, Mericourt-l'Abbe, France. He was twenty-two. He was my uncle.

Bob Curry

Christmas present in the trenches.
A clip of .303 ammunition.

The Commonwealth War Graves Commission tends graves and memorials to 1.75-million servicemen and women at 23,000 different locations in 150 countries.

The atom bomb

Letters to my sister Pixie (Dr Margaret Stanfield)

Sian, China, August 8, 1945.

We are in the middle of the hot (and I mean hot) season . . . days between 100-110C, nights about 95C. In fact, too hot for comfort. The heat brought out the scorpions and we killed five one night in my room and odd numbers since. Horrible looking beasts and very painful, so I am told. I am certainly very careful when getting into bed.

I have just made up a solution of DDT and hope it will discourage them somewhat, but am doubtful. I think they are a little large. I am, at the moment, feeding on sulphaguanadine as I have had a few bouts of dysentery.

I have had a smack at the flies in the kitchen with DDT! Their population has been reduced by at least 100 times . . . as far as bed bugs go, it is apparently their favourite food. Talking of food I am eating two Chinese meals and an English breakfast per day. Unfortunately, what made the Chinese meals so acceptable, water melons, are now banned throughout China for fear of cholera.

In our house (on August 10, 1945) Mr Ho laid on a dinner for various high Chinese officials, the Governor of the Province, the second in command of the War Zone, the Governor of the Bank of China etc. Mrs Ho arranged the dinner and afterwards we sat out on the patio.

There was some shouting on the streets and Ho sent the boy out to find out what was happening. He returned with a news sheet. The Japanese had surrendered. The Atom Bomb had destroyed Hiroshima.

Sian, August 11, 1945.

We heard the news of the atomic bombs last night on one of my sets. It has certainly come suddenly . . but I don't blame the Japs with atomic bombs buzzing around. The Chinese newspapers are saying that the crater is nearly a mile deep!

John Stanfield

Chapter 11

Home and Family

Keep the home fires burning
while your hearts are yearning.
LENA GUILBERT FORD, 1918

Danger in Digbeth

John Carmichael came to Birmingham from Argyll to join Birmingham City Police as Constable No. A78 in March 1938. He was 19 and, before he joined the Army in 1942, he was right in the centre of the worst of the blitz. He had one or two lucky escapes from death which rained down from the skies.

The first part of the war was fairly docile and we plodded on with routine duties - booking the odd person for breaches of blackout regulations and catching the odd thief.

In 1941, however, the pace hotted up and the Birmingham area received many heavy bomb and incendiary attacks. The raid on Coventry was spectacular and I watched it from the roof of Digbeth Police Station where I was, although officially off duty, on fire watch. The next morning, at 6 am, with many others I was on my way to Coventry to help the citizens and to prevent looting. Not a big raid by the standard of some that were to come later, but the concentration of damage and loss of life was immense. I did duty in Earlsdon for several days, bunking down in a church hall.

Meantime the pace hotted up in Birmingham with some very heavy raids on the city centre and the Digbeth and Deritend area, no doubt meant for the GWR viaduct. I can't remember them hitting it but they put the fear of God into those who lived there.

We always knew in advance when a "red alert" was on the way, but the weird wailing note of the sirens gave you a few collywobbles.

Many buildings around the area were destroyed or damaged. I remember being on duty in Smallbrook Street when a mass of incendiary bombs set most of the street alight, including the Empire Theatre at the corner of Hurst Street. I well remember the licensee of the Long Bar in Smallbrook Street, which was well alight, exhorting a group of soldiers to help themselves quickly before it all went up in flames. A few minutes later, at the junction with Worcester Street, I found a middle-aged man lying in the road with both legs blown off and other injuries. He died on the way to hospital.

Memories come flooding back: New Street blocked by the collapse of the front of Marshall and Snelgrove and the big shopping arcade nearby; seeing a land mine floating down on its parachute and landing in Heath Mill Lane, off Deritend, with a blinding explosion causing enormous damage to property and causing severe loss of life; having to attend the scene of another land mine explosion in Benacre Street, running between Sherlock Street and Bristol Street, The damage was tremendous with about 40 lives lost, many injured, and 300 homes demolished or so badly damaged that they were pulled down.

It was here that an old lady whose house, although some way from the epicentre of the explosion, but still badly damaged, was found very concerned over the safety of her budgie which was in its cage in the front bedroom.

I managed to mount the badly damaged stairs and, to her joy, found the bird quite chirpy and hopping about in its cage. I brought it down and she was overjoyed, gave me a big hug, and went off to live with her daughter.

On the same morning, about 5.30 am, an old market lady trudged along Sherlock Street, heading for the Bull Ring and her market stall. Some life did go on fairly normally despite the disruption. She surveyed the remains of the branch of the Birmingham Municipal Bank and declared: " . . . kept telling them not to put their money in them places. All gone up in bleedin' smoke now!"

Digbeth Police Station continued to be rather close to the action and, on a particular evening, I was one of the PCs retained in the station to be dispatched to any incident. I was in the mess room when there was an almighty explosion. The lights went out and the whole building shook.

A large bomb (500 lbs.) had struck immediately between the station and John Morgan's Pork Butchers next door who proclaimed "Fresh Sausages Every Hour". Johnny's slaughterhouse was badly damaged as well as parts of the police station.

On going to investigate I thought a number of people had been killed. Fortunately the carnage was the remains of about ten pigs which had been awaiting slaughter the next day!

I thought that was a near squeak, but nothing to compare with something that happened a few nights later.

A very heavy raid was in progress and I was posted in the Sherlock Street area, away beyond the Meat Market in Cheapside. The din from bombs, the ack-ack guns - many close to the city centre in parks such as Calthorpe Park - added to the general confusion caused by a large number of fires.

It is difficult to remember times. Most raids started about 7 pm and went on till perhaps midnight or even into the small hours of the morning. But there was a lull and the inspector in charge told me to take the opportunity to go and get something to eat in the Station and make a cup of tea. I went into the station kitchen and was in the process of filling the tea pot when Inspector Nicholls came in and, at that instant, I heard a loud fluctuating "whooshing" noise, followed by a violent impact. The building shook and the lights went out.

We went out into the road and an elderly sergeant proclaimed in the light of his diffused torch that "a part of Johnny Morgan's sausage machine was lying on his counter."

To our surprise and horror it turned out to have German wording on its side. It was, in fact, a German land mine which had come off its parachute and had come down tumbling over and over and this was what had probably prevented its detonation.

If it had gone off I would not be writing this today since it would have cleared an area of about 300 yards in each direction. Immediately the Police Station was evacuated and for three or four days we slept on the floor in various rooms in Steelhouse Lane Police Station while the Royal Navy devised means of rendering it harmless.

They were very much afraid that if it had gone off part of the GWR viaduct would have been demolished with delays to defence equipment travelling that route.

I could go on for a very long time yet about things that happened around this "at risk" police station. But one sad incident was the death of a very likeable policeman, PC Bertie Brady, a former member of the Household Cavalry and a native of Abertillery, Glamorgan. Like others he had come in for a short break and a cup of tea. I was in the Station but not in the mess room when an anti-personnel bomb landed in Allison Street and burst on impact. Shrapnel penetrated the sandbags protecting the mess room windows and struck him on the forehead, killing him instantly.

John Carmichael

From evacuee . . .
When war was declared on September 3, 1939, I was already in South Wales having been evacuated on September 1.

Hundreds of children were on Snow Hill Station (Birmingham), each with a label sewn or pinned on to an outer garment. Teachers and helpers checked off our names, and put a number on our label. We were all clutching a gas mask and extra clothing in an assortment of ways: battered cases, paper carrier bags, parcels tied up with string, etc. Eventually we got on a train at 7.30 am and away we went - to where we knew not. About six hours later we arrived at a small town station to be told we were in Abergavenny. At least we could pronounce it.

After much commanding and counter-commanding by the teachers and helpers in charge of us we were loaded on to buses with numbers corresponding to the numbers on our labels. We were given 24-hour rations. These consisted of a tin of corned beef, a tin of peas, a small bag of potatoes, a packet of tea and sugar, a tin of condensed milk, two bread buns, a pat of butter, a small packet of biscuits, an apple, an orange, and a bar of chocolate. We assumed that if we got surrounded by Germans we could eat the rations to save them falling into enemy hands and throw the tins at them!

Having boarded the coaches, we proceeded to a village called Pandy. In the village hall we were assigned to our different billets - all this done without councillors, childminders, welfare people or the DHSS!

My best friend Peggy and I were fortunate in being assigned to a Mr and Mrs Probert who owned a farm at the base of the Black Mountain range in a parish called Oldcastle, just over the mountain from Llantony Abbey. The farm was called Oldcastle Court, or I should say, it is still called that.

For some children the evacuation lasted only a matter of a few days or weeks because they were so unhappy or, in some cases, so badly treated that they preferred the city and the bombing rather than to stay where they were.

As I have said, Peggy and I were fortunate for we were about to start some of the happiest days of our lives. At least I was. Peggy, after about 18 months, didn't stay the course either.

At first Peggy and I had a three mile walk to school in Pandy and, of course, back again in the afternoon. The Probert boys (Ces and Will) along with the children from two other nearby farms were taken to and from school in a taxi. The Parish Council, in their infinite wisdom, decided that "as the War would be over by Christmas" it wasn't worth altering the system for two evacuees. Fortunately, just after new Year, 1940, when the weather got very bad they relented.

The food we had was marvellous: Freshly baked bread, home-made butter and cheese, new-laid eggs, hams and sides of pork hanging from the kitchen ceiling - a kitchen which was about 20 feet square.

There was no electricity - all oil lamps and candles; no indoor plumbing, so you carried your big jug of cold water up every night for your wash; only hip baths in your room and you had to carry your own hot water up when you wanted a *full* wash.

And, of course, the toilet . . .

Now this is something to write about. It was called a Ty-Bach, Little House or the "Petty". It could also have been called a "friendly toilet" being a two-seater. It was a very solid brick construction build about a foot above a mountain stream half way down the garden. (I've always made it a policy never to drink mountain water). Of course it was not too bad in summer and the reading material was usually up to date and, if you could get a full story, quite good. But the winter was something else, especially in the middle of the night when the candle would blow out. You've heard of "bum freezer weather"? Well, this was it.

We had been there just over 12 months when I had a rather nasty accident and acquired my war wounds! I fell out of an apple tree on to a three strand barbed wire fence and ripped all down the back of my left leg.

I was carried into the farmhouse covered in blood. Mrs Probert proceeded to pour iodine all down my leg and I passed out, only to come round and hear her say to send for Mr Evans the local butcher.

In his spare time he went round the farms and slaughtered the pigs for the farmers' own use. So I wasn't too happy at the thought of him coming to see me. I thought, "he's going to cut my leg off or kill me." What I had not known was that he was also the local First Aid expert, called before the doctor in Abergavenny. For several weeks after I was thoroughly spoiled and basked in the glory of it.

As time passed I went to Abergavenny grammar School and, by now, I was treated as a member of the family. Mr Probert was now "Uncle Will" and Mrs Probert "Mama". I had also been given a horse to ride, so my school days were idyllic.

...to Land Girl

At sixteen and a half I was ready to leave school. Uncle Will decided that the Land Girl he had would have to go as she was useless. So, after he had written a lot of letters on my behalf, in 1943 I was allowed to join the Women's Land Army (WLA). I got a nice new uniform, work clothes and, after my "keep" was taken, I had ten shillings (50p) a month to spend on frivolities and pleasure!

The work was extremely hard, up at 4.30 am and working until it was too dark for us to see. In the summer, at harvest time, we would be out in the fields from sun-up until sun-down. Food and drink would be brought out to us in the form of a picnic, and marvellous it was. By bed-time I didn't go to sleep - I collapsed into bed and fell into a coma.

My real moment of fame at work came with "Whitehouse William", a pedigree Hereford bull. He weighed about one and a half tons and I was the only one who could handle him. If Uncle Will or Davy (the farm labourer)wanted to do anything with him, they had to use "the pole". This was a long rod with a hook on the end which would go through the ring in Bill's nose, and hope for the best. But he would stand me holding the ring and leading him anywhere.

A couple of years after I left I took Jeff, my husband, to the farm. Bill had retired but I went to his field and called him and he remembered me.

Of course, we had our mad times. Like when we were returning late on a summer evening with the last load of hay. I was riding on top of the load, Davy took the steep slope too acutely and the load went over with me underneath. Not at all pleasant to be buried under sweet smelling hay. Also, when we had the new tractor, I was allowed to have a test drive. I panicked and finished up with the front wheels in the ditch.

But I think one of the funniest times was when the "cider man" came around to pulp our apples. The apples were left over winter in the Old Mill to "season" a little. The mill had no roof; birds used to peck them over and the wasps feed on them. It was open to the elements. Whatever there was was shovelled into the cider press; the horse hair mats were indescribable, but, after the cider had matured, it was delicious.

The pulp after the pressing was left a couple of days before we cleaned up. We came back from some job and found the old sow who had had a delightful meal of them, was absolutely legless (or should I say "trotterless"?) and was lying there in a stupor. We then had the job of getting a hefty sow in farrow into a wheel barrow and back to her sty. Not a pleasant job at all. She was "out" and every time we tried to move her she had terrible wind problems. I can remember the hysterics it caused but I am glad to say that the litter she finally produced was lovely.

Davy, the labourer, was an idle devil. He would find any excuse to sleep under a hedge during the day. This was because of his nightly visit to the Pandy Hotel, getting home in the early hours. In spite of this he was still allowed to sit with us for meals where a running battle ensued every meal time between him and Mama.

She used to put margarine instead of butter (because she reckoned he couldn't tell the difference and that was good enough for him) by his place and she would keep the butter at her end of the table. It made no difference to Davy. He just walked the length of the table and took the dish back to his end. Uncle Will finally took charge and said the nonsense had to stop: in future it would be either butter or marg for all of us. Thank goodness Mama thought marg as fit only for axle grease or she might have battled on.

As you can imagine, I had a good war and was sorry when, in 1946, my father said I had to return home. I hated working in an office. So, for quite some time, I returned as often as I could at week-ends.

Vicky Hollins

Black Market

Prior to the war most of the rural towns and villages had their own butcher, baker, grocer, greengrocer, and so on. My town was no exception. With a population of 5,000 we had several private butchers, plus the Co-op.

Quite a lot of people had their own pens where they would keep a dozen or so laying hens; some would have a sty to keep a pig.

Most of the butchers had a slaughterhouse at the rear of their premises, often with a small field and stabling, or a small barn or shed in which to keep the animals before killing. They provided a service to the pig owners in addition to their own requirements.

With the onset of war a rationing system was devised. Each animal had to be registered in order to obtain a permit to provide food for the animal and a licence to slaughter. The large towns and cities had abbatoirs with strict controls in order to ration the available meat. This was sold at a controlled price with the ration varying, depending on the supply situation. It fluctuated between 1s 2p. and 1s 11d. per person per week. Each family had to register with their preferred butcher.

This created a massive black market with each butcher anxious to please his customers and almost all customers pleased to obtain a little extra to feed their families. Often animals were not registered. They were fed on scraps and grazing until being slaughtered, either at the small butchers or out in a barn in the country.

This was against the law.

However, with one food inspector who was also probably the health inspector, to cover a large country area, very few prosecutions took place. Most people did not consider this to be wrong, hence the loveable Spiv of Dad's Army. I did hear of a butcher who was sent to prison. He was made the victualling officer for the prison for the period of his sentence.

In my case, as a lad of 15 in 1939, I was a butcher's boy for 48 hours a week; a message boy for the ARP control centre on every fourth night from 10 pm until 7 am; two nights at school; one night at Scouts; one night at the ATC teaching Morse Code to beginners and acting as the "enemy" for the Home Guard on Sundays.

But there was still plenty of time to feed a sty of six pigs and look after 200 cockerels from August to December, fattening them up for Christmas. The *six* pigs were registered as *one*, which meant that I received only enough pig meal for one animal. As the pigs were owned by a prominent and respected director of the large company I worked for, this did not create a problem. Each week a number of bags of broken biscuits would arrive from the biscuit factory. This, together with the vegetable scraps from the greengrocer and the restaurant, meant good feeding for the pigs.

Do you remember the film *The Private Function*? This was true to life for me.

I was now 16 and well into 1940. The director obtained a licence (not dated) to kill his *one* pig . The routine was that on a Friday night a van driver would take me to the sty. I would have to select the pig to be killed quietly with a "stun hammer". This was a large ball point hammer with a hollow point opposite the ball. Without going into too much detail, the pig was stunned before killing, after which it was loaded into the van and taken into the slaughterhouse where, by candlelight behind blackout curtains, the carcass was shaved with boiling water prior to hanging over the week-end.

On Monday morning the pig was cut into joints and wrapped in greaseproof paper. The director would arrive in his chauffeur-driven Daimler, complete with a large travelling rug. He would take his chauffeur into the office, leaving the car outside the slaughterhouse. I packed the pork on the back seat wrapped in the travelling rug. The director would return, sit on the pork, and drive off to his office in Manchester.

For this risky task I was rewarded with the princely sum of 6d. I often wondered how much my boss received for allowing me to do this work.

This was repeated at intervals until the last pig had been declared as per the licence. Then the routine would start all over again.

Poultry were legitimate. I fed them until the week before Christmas when we had to kill them with our fingers and pluck them ready for the customers' Christmas Dinner. This continued until 1942. I was then 18 and able to join the Royal Navy in November.

I escaped from the killing of Civvy street to the peace of war.

Norman Schofield

Anderson shelter

The yard of shipbuilders and engineers Vickers Armstrong Ltd was at Barrow-in-Furness which launched 200 vessels between September 1924 and March 1945. Some 137 of these were commissioned by the Royal Navy. 114 were submarines and the surface vessels included the aircraft carriers HMS Illustrious, built in 1939, and HMS Indomitable in 1940.

Barrow had a liberal share of action on the Home Front.

The day war broke out I was almost three and a half years old, an age old enough to accept the excitement of the time, but too young to appreciate the horror of the events and the fears and anxieties of my parents and family.

My first memory is of an interrupted night and being carried down to the newly constructed air raid shelter in the back yard. In later years I mused on the logic of such a structure. I would have thought that if the house had received a direct hit then the shelter would have been involved.

It is worth pointing out that Anderson Shelters were not possible in "Coronation Street style" back-to-back terraces and so were an "out-house."

One memory which stays with me is the smell of new bricks and mortar. Whenever I have occasion to enter a a newly-constructed or partially completed building, that memory returns. It reminds me of the night I was awoken in the shelter by the resounding bang of a direct hit only a few hundred yards away. Although it was a frightening experience the real horror of what was happening did not register.

My home in 14 Clifford Street faced the fire station and one might imagine the degree of disturbance caused even with the shelter at the rear of the terrace.

My maternal grandfather had retired after a life in the shipyard. In an effort to maintain his involvement in the work of the yard he loved so much he would use me as an excuse (much like some men do with a dog in an effort to visit the pub), and take me in the push chair to the bridge which crossed the fitting out basin and repair yard and then make an assessment of the "state of play".

One occasion, I remember distinctly, was the sight of *HMS Illustrious* in the dock for a rapid repair. The same evening the town received a more hostile visit as a consequence.   On another occasion my grandfather would use counting practice as a pretence to assess what vessels were around. He "helped" me to count over 30 submarines in dock.

On a sunny Sunday morning I was pushed to the usual destination and witnessed the shelling of a lone and possibly crippled Dornier bomber, nicknamed the "flying pencil" because of its long and slim fuselage. The puffs of white cloud appeared round it, but on that occasion it was the one that got away.

In 1942 my family was evacuated to the Coniston area of the Lake District, to a cottage on the border of farmland and fell. There is an irony in these memories. The war provided me and my brother with three very happy and educative years. For example, there were long warm summers, haymaking and harvest time, with glorious farmhouse teas brought to the field by the farmer's wife, hayrides, fishing for trout with an ash branch and line, predictable winters and unlimited sledging and, above all, a greater knowledge of and respect for wild life. My family experienced the hardships and consequence of war as we returned to our bomb damaged home. And yet, unknowingly, we acquired the will to succeed and overcome.

Malcolm Allen

Anderson Shelters were designed and put into production before war broke out in September 1939. The Government had made assessments on the potential risk from bombing based on the blitz of Barcelona in March 1938. For each ton of high explosive munitions dropped on a congested area it was estimated that it would cost approximately 50 casualties.

It was decided to offer initial protection to 2.5-million families (12-million people) at a cost of £20-million. The shelters, designed to be surface shelters with the base sunk two to three feet deep and the rest covered by soil or sandbags, consisted of 14 corrugated iron sheets weighing about 8 cwt. The tops of the main support sheets were curved to provide greater strength and they could be bolted together to form an arch.

The standard structure was 6 ft. high, 4 ft. 6 ins wide, and 6 ft. 6 ins. long and could accommodate four people comfortably, and six at a pinch. The shelter was not considered to be bomb proof, especially against a direct hit, but offered protection from debris. Although many shelters were given free to poor families they were sold, frequently on instalments, from £6. 14s (£6.70p) to £10. 18s. (£10.90p)

In the UK, 457,000 houses were destroyed during the blitz and another 4-million damaged.

A War Widow

The church bells were celebrating the end of the war when Sally was born on my first wedding anniversary, April 19, 1945. Her father had been posted missing by Bomber Command in August 1944 and presumed dead when Sally was three months old.

He did not know that he was to be a father.

Sally was brought up with my three sisters and my parents who considered her to be daughter number five. She was a very strong minded and determined child with an over-riding interest in and love of animals. She naturally wanted to be a vet but, because of asthma, she was advised not to take up the career. However, she became an air hostess and was flying at the age of 18, emulating her father, and was filmed by Blue Peter as the youngest air hostess in the country.

It was as an air hostess that she met and married her husband, Richard, a civil engineer and lived for a short period in Jamaica before settling in the United Kingdom and eventually in Tenterden, Kent. Simon, her son, was born shortly after they returned to England.

When Sally was diagnosed as having Non-Hodgkinson Lymphoma disease she was determined that the illness would in no way alter her life or that of others, in particular her immediate family.

As her condition deteriorated she became pro-active in helping others with the same illness, raising money for research, assisting the medical staff in understanding the patient's attitude towards the illness, and counselling other patients. It was during this period that she received radio and chemo-therapy treatment and underwent several operations with fortitude and without complaint. It was a credit to Sally's courage and tenacity that at no time did she allow her illness to interfere with her work, helping others, or her love for the wild animals who regularly visited her home.

Typical of Sally's pragmatic view of life was that, when she finally realised and accepted that she was fighting a loosing battle, she insisted on arranging her affairs in detail, including her funeral. Her consideration of others did not falter. She approached death with magnanimity and dignity saying not only would she meet her Heavenly Father but she would meet her own father for the first time and they would always be near me.

Sally, in her last years of life, had been making extensive inquiries into the circumstances of her father's death. His Lancaster bomber failed to return from a raid over Konigsberg, Germany. The aircraft crashed on German territory (now Russian territory) but no information has ever been received as to the whereabouts of the crew or their final resting place.

Her inquiries had reached as far afield as Russia and Canada and, though progress had been slow, a gradual picture was being built up; she was very optimistic of the outcome and had planned to visit the crash site. Sally did not live to fulfil her plans.

Sally was not without a sense of humour. She often supported me at War Widows meetings where she would remark that the mothers were wearing better than their daughters. She said that it must be the effects of living with domineering mothers.

This small premature child, my daughter, became a courageous compassionate woman, wife, and mother who, for me, replaced her father.

Marjorie Gay

From time to time, as Secretary of 619 Squadron Association, I receive enquiries from relatives about crew members who were posted missing, presumed killed in action. The Squadron Operations Record Book, which I hold, contains a complete record of every operation undertaken by the Squadron during World War 11. It includes the Squadron letter and number of each aircraft, the names of each crew member flying in the aircraft, the time of take-off and landing and the individual crew report following debriefing.

I am often able to provide the relatives with pieces of information of which they were unaware.

Mrs Marjorie Gay, an Associate Member of the Squadron Association, and widow of Flying Officer D.F. Gay, sent me the very moving article about her daughter Sally, which has appeared in *Courage* the War Widows' Newsletter.

Flying Officer Gay and his crew were posted missing after the operation by 619 Squadron to Konigsberg, Baltic Sea, (now Kalingrad, Russia) on August 29-30, 1944. The crew were operating from RAF Dunholme Lodge, a bomber airfield about five miles north east of Lincoln, in Lancaster 111 PG-M, LM 656. The Operations Record Book states: "Missing: nothing heard from this aircraft subsequent to take-off at 20.36 hrs."

John Whiteley

From one blitz to another

What strange coincidences there are as one goes through life.

Mine arose out of the Spanish Civil War when I was a child and the Germans terrorised the cities of northern Spain by bombing and killing thousands of people. This helped the Germans to gain experience for what was to come in the Second World War.

Because of the blitz I was fortunate in being sent to England.

To experience a war in one's lifetime is bad enough. But *two wars* is hell!

I came to Coventry in the summer of 1940 at the age of 16 and I found work in a munitions factory. In September of that year Coventry experienced its first taste of the blitz, warning us that wars are not only fought on the battlefields, and that air raids would come to be a way of life for the city.

The daily routine for the people of Coventry became: sleep when possible between raids, work long shifts and work seven days per week. If you were working night shift, and the air raid warning sounded, everyone went to their designated post such as firewatching.

Somehow, despite all this, we found time for enjoyment including football, swimming and dancing.

One night I was at the Scala Cinema when the siren sounded. It was customary to stay put as the odds of a bomb falling on the cinema were rare. But the noise of the bombs exploding were getting closer. So I decided to go home which was just as well. Soon afterwards a bomb fell on the cinema killing over 200 people.

Life in Coventry was hard at that time, but never in my life have I experienced a city with such determination, unity and comradeship and with one objective, the defeat of the enemy.

Alfredo Ruiz

In the massive raid on Coventry on November 14, 1940, 554 people were killed and another 865 were seriously injured. The raid by 500 bombers began at 7.20 pm and lasted for eleven hours. During that time they dropped 503 tons of high explosives and 881 incendiary bombs on the city.

My Boer War link

I joined the 13/18 Royal Hussars (Queen Mary's Own) in 1926 at Edinburgh. Then, in 1927-28, Lord Baden-Powell, the Honorary Colonel of the Regiment, made a presentation to every member, a tobacco tin embossed with the Regimental insignia, making contact with everyone.

I was honoured to shake hands with the ex-commander of the troops from the Boer War.

I still have the tin and treasure the memory of the mounted march past.

Bert Hallett

Mr Hallett, who was born in 1907, is a member of Napton & District Royal British Legion Branch. He served as the local policeman for many years, supporting both the Parish, local charities, sport and youth.

All part of war

I was bombed out of five different offices in Plymouth. Typewriters became so scarce I carried a heavy portable typewriter home to Saltash with me every night and brought it back in the morning. The bus station was flattened and we had virtually no buses and, at one stage, I walked the five miles to the Ferry to cross the river - complete with my typewriter - the rail lines having been hit, and then back gain in the morning. It was all part of war.

I well remember seeing the "little boats" coming in from the Dunkirk evacuation with soldiers in such a sorry state and passing them my sandwich lunch.

As I tried to get to my office one day I found the road was cordoned off. I stood looking at it wondering if there was another way round when suddenly an unexploded bomb went off. A man, a complete stranger, threw me to the ground with himself on top. We were both all right apart from being somewhat shaken.

Plymouth was, of course, a Naval city with a dockyard so, I suppose, it was a legitimate target.

Every day I found time to write to my husband. I also joined the Women's Voluntary Service, worked in the Service Canteens, and manned telephones at Air Raid Report Centres. I wonder how I found the time. But my mother kept the home fires burning and my father worked in a railway signal box. One worked all the hours there were with very little sleep due to the air raids.

Five people with whom I worked were killed one night in their shelter. They were all musical, got together in a little quintet they had formed and hopped off to their shelter when the sirens sounded, only to receive a direct hit. In the room they had vacated the music was still on the stands.

Eventually a post became vacant, at Saltash where I lived, in an evacuation office dealing with evacuees from Plymouth, London, Coventry and Birmingham.

After a few months I was in charge with two other girls working with me. This was a job I enjoyed very much, trying to sort out problems. And there were many. Some evacuees were unaccompanied children, but mostly they were mothers with children. Saltash was not itself a reception area but the rural district was. I was just 20 and didn't drive, but we were supposed to use drivers and cars from a car pool.

Iris Herwin

Brothers in arms

Four brothers from one Warwickshire village, Napton, went to war and served their country. Only one returned unscathed.

Stanley Sheasby enlisted in the Royal Artillery in 1941 and served, mainly in the Middle East, until he was invalided home on April 18, 1943.

Johnnie Sheasby joined the RAF and was killed on August 16, 1940 during an enemy bombing raid on Tangmere, Sussex, during the Battle of Britain.

Job Sheasby, an amateur boxer before he joined the Army, had been in Singapore for just three days before the surrender on February 15, 1942 when more than 70,000 British and Commonwealth troops were captured. He spent three years as a POW and worked as a slave labourer on the notorious Burma Railway.
When released he weighted only 84 lbs and had lost some fingers during captivity. He always refused to talk about his experiences.

Bower Sheasby, who joined the RAF and served in Calcutta, was the only one who suffered no injuries and returned home safely.

I wrote this poem when I heard that Johnnie had died in an air raid during the Battle of Britain.

It is almost two months
since we learned of your death;
But we still can't believe it's true,
Why should God take
Who was one of the best
Four brothers - and one of them you.

Remembrance is clear,
For it was not long ago
That last evening, together we spent
You had just volunteered for the Air Force and so
Came to wish us goodbye as you went.

How with envy we thrilled
As we listened with awe
To the tale of the deeds you had heard,
Deeds performed by the men
In whose trials you would share
As they soared through the air like a bird.

There are three of us now
To continue the fight
So, depend on us - don't dismay
You have given your life
For a cause to defend
And now - we've our own debt to pay.

That is why it seems very hard
That an error of time
Should snuff out your life like a flame
It wasn't as though
You were given a chance
The worth of your name.

It may be a task
To dismiss that you've gone
But this we must do - must not brood
For there is not a man
Of courage and pride
Who could fight in the dullness of mood.

Please forgive us old pal
If it is good-bye for now
We hope this conveys how we feel
Women cry good and hard
But we are men, and that's barred
So we will take in our stride - a raw deal.

His smile we shall always remember
His voice we still seem to hear
We know he is safe in God's keeping
But oh, how we all miss him dear.

We gather the flowers of remembrance,
The best that our hearts can frame
We weave them into a garland
And entwine them around his name.

Stanley Sheasby

Civilian 'white flag'

ARGENTINE REPUBLIC
Malvinas Operation Theatre Command, Communique No 3.
Instructions for the Population

As a consequence of all the necessary actions taken, and in order to ensure the safety of the population, all people are to remain at their homes until further notice. New instructions will be issued.

The population must bear in mind that, in order to ensure the fulfilment of these instructions, military troops shall arrest all people found outside their homes.

To avoid inconvenience and personal misfortunes, people are to abide by the following:

1. Should some serious problem arise and people wish to make it known to the military authorities, a white piece of cloth is to be placed outside the door. Military patrols will visit the house so as to be informed and provide a solution.

2. All schools, shops, stores, banks, pubs and clubs are to remain closed until further notice.

3. All infringements shall be treated according to what is stated in EDICT No 1.

4. All further instructions shall be released through the local broadcasting station which shall remain in permanent operation.

ISLAS MALVINAS 02Abr 1982

Osvaldo Jorge Carcia - General
Commandante del Teatro de Operaciones
Malvinas.

I found this curfew notice still pinned to a doorway in Port Stanley after the Argentine surrender on June 14, 1982. It carried the date of the Argentine invasion three months earlier and, obviously, as an afterthought, the invaders recognised that civilians might have to break the curfew in an emergency.

Nevertheless, they still took the opportunity to impose a symbol of humiliation on the hostile and resentful population by insisting on a white flag being displayed.

255 Britons and 652 Argentines died in the conflict.

Aubrey Chalmers

Building the Legion Club

Immediately after the end of the Second World War the Knowle and District Branch of the Royal British Legion set about providing a permanent home, headquarters and club. As early as October 1944 the possibility of purchasing US Army huts in Station Road was considered.

A building fund was launched and various options were considered. Eventually the present site in Station Road was obtained and site work began around 1951. The building work such as labouring was carried out by volunteer Branch members with some professional guidance. The premises opened in 1954 and, since then, extensions have been added to produce one of the most luxurious clubs.

Sunday morning had arrived. 9.30 was the time.

Dad was there, Lilian and I, and my boyfriend at that time, Brian Stephens, was also there with his tractor ready to start to pull the hedge out.

We were in the grounds and a pathway was made. Then the fun began. The shed was put up for the cement, a pit was dug for the lime, plans looked at, the footings pegged out. The rain came down and filled the footings. Lillian and I had an old stirrup pump and we took turns until we had them ready for the brickies to start building.

The first brickies were Charlie Ryder and George Burton being kept supplied with cement by Don Price, Alec Callow and Joe Higgs (Honorary member) on the mixer. And when you think of it all the men who helped on the site had their own jobs during the day. Don Price then rode his bike from Sheldon and back at night, every night that was. It took some doing.

Lillian, Mom and I unloaded the first bricks and one driver showed us how to catch them and stack them. I remember Mom going to fetch Dad gone 12 o'clock. He was still at work with a hurricane lamp.

The Army came on a Saturday and Sunday afternoon, the Engineers, to put in the girders so that the roof could go on. Colonel Patterson laid on a meal for them along with the men on the site, at the Red Lion.

The thing that I remember is the laughter that went on, Don Price drowning Joe Higgs many times with buckets of water while cleaning the mixer at night. Poor old Don, his glasses got steamed up and Joe got it every time. We kept out of the way.

It would be nice to have a plaque to these men who gave up their time for the Club and Branch. Never mind. Their names are in a sealed bottle in the foundations along with the Daily Mirror (Jane. Remember her?) and coins of the realm.

Mom was the first cleaner. It was hard work, polishing on her hands and knees for a long time until Les Moulston got her a floor polisher. Mom went back at night to get the fire going so it was warm for everyone. After Thursday nights she did not like the floor next morning. Beer was spilt on it and made it awful to polish.

Happy days!

Beryl Pratt

Chapter 12

Christmas

With the poor, the mean, and lowly,
Lived on earth our Saviour Holy.
TRADITIONAL CAROL

Stalag V111b.

Nov.30, 1942. Stalag V111b surely is the most dreadful of all prison camps. We do our best to remain cheerful, but I am afraid it is only a poor best. We commence to decorate the barrack with silver paper stars and Happy Christmas etc.

Dec. 17, '42. I haven't looked forward to a Christmas more than this one, as far as I can remember. This is not strange really for we all look forward to 1943 which, I feel sure, will be our year of victory. Of even more importance to us right now is that we hope soon to receive a Christmas Red Cross parcel. This should stave off our perpetual feeling of hunger for at least a couple of days. Have been planning what I shall do with the contents of the parcel, how I shall eat it, that is, for the last two months!

It would appear that I was obsessed with food but, looking back, I don't think it was so. We rarely, if ever, had enough to eat and quite often would go days without eating or drinking. But, provided one was able to concentrate one's mind on other subjects, food took second place. When we were restricted in chains under heavy guard, of course there was less incentive to exercise one's mind profitably.

Dec. 21, '42. The Hun Christmas celebrations commence today and, because of this, we are unchained a little early. We had a concert in 17b. Quite good. The Hun guards complain that they are having no extra rations this week - a good thing! One guard tells me he has not been home to his wife and family for three years!

Dec. 23, '42. Our parcels arrive today. Shall need to keep a sharp eye on mine to avoid its walking away! The weather remains good with very severe frosts. Contents of parcel. 2 oz. milk, 4 oz. chocolate, 1 lb. steak and tomatoes. 1 lb. steak and macaroni. 3 oz. cheese. 4 oz. sweets. half lb. choc. biscuits. tin of jam. 2 oz. tea. tablet of soap. 6 oz. sugar. 1 lb. cake. half lb. butter, and 1 lb. Christmas pudding. Fortunately - miraculously - the parcels were unopened, i.e. tins not pierced.

Dec. 24, '42. We have been issued with 50 cigarettes for Christmas week. Bought a 4 oz. bar of chocolate yesterday for 30 cigarettes. Had Soper decorate a Christmas card for Jimmy - with our signatures.

The Commandant has sent us greetings and hopes we won't be here next year - we won't be chum, don't worry - 1943 and victory.

We are unchained in the evening and allowed out of the compound for a little while. There is even music on the public address system. The beer is broached - pretty poor stuff - followed by a sing song. Find it difficult not to be wistful. Am wondering how my darling is - how she will spend Christmas. My thoughts will be only of her and I pray she will be joyful. God bless you sweetheart. Later Christmas Eve. Murder.

The amplifiers of the public address system were attached high up to the poles carrying the electricity cables. They were used only for propaganda purposes.

The camp housed prisoners from scores of - possibly a hundred - different countries. Similarly there were numerous religions, and, to some of those devout men, Christianity was either unheard of or actively derogated. Murder within the camp was not uncommon, and the fact that one occurred on a Christmas Eve was not a particularly noteworthy event.

POWs ate, slept and used the same overcrowded billets for recreation. These remarkable pictures, taken secretly inside Stalag V111b, were kept by Eric Herwin throughout captivity and preserved even during the death march

Dec. 25, '42. Christmas Day. For the first time my hunger is fully satisfied though, half an hour later, I'm as hungry as ever, due possibly to four months of semi-starvation. Jack and I wangle a box of raw potatoes for 10 cigarettes. The Huns have reduced their food ration to us this holiday. If I hadn't saved some food, and didn't have a Christmas box of food, I'd be in a sorry state.

Menu:
Breakfast. Potato crisp with milk and sugar, bread, margarine and apricot jam, tea and chocolate.
Lunch. Potato and cheese pie, bread, margarine and jam. A little Hun fishpaste and ersatz honey, chocolate and candies.
Dinner. Mash potato, tinned steak and tomato, Christmas pudding, cake and biscuits.

We were awakened by the carol singers this morning. About 25% of the chaps have been violently ill during the past two days. My tummy has been rumbling, threateningly. Our stomachs are unused to good food and just cannot cope.

Eric Herwin

POW's Christmas Card drawn in Stalag V111b, Christmas 1942.

Western Desert

The 8th Army was pushing west towards Tobruk to relieve the garrison which had been besieged for several months. It was in the middle of December 1941 when we formed up outside Tobruk and went in two or three days before Christmas.

We took over a gunfight which had been occupied during the siege and were soon ready for action. It was a case of moving into the various dugouts round the gun emplacements and making them reasonably habitable. They had been cut into the sandstone with a deep section in the middle and, on three sides, ledges about three feet wide on which we slept.

Our site was close to an old fort which now housed various stores and the cookhouse.

On Christmas Day we had corned beef fritters and tinned potatoes followed by tinned pineapple as a bit of a treat.

That morning a small party of us went into Tobruk to attend the church service. The church was filled with numbers of various units stationed around. We stood quite tightly packed as, of course, any form of seating had long since gone.

Looking up one could see large expanses of blue sky where the roof was missing, hoping that there would be no interruptions from the Stukas. Maybe the Luftwaffe was taking a day off.

The service was led by a Padre wearing a rather torn surplice over his battledress. We sang carols and thought of home, after which we hurried back into our transport and returned to our various units.

Fred Frost

Korean POW Camp

Local concert parties were put on at Christmas in the town's cinema by each company. The place was frozen but everyone struggled to get a place at each of the seven company concerts.

All the material had to be passed by the Chinese censors. Much of it they could not or would not understand.

For 7 Company's concert I once gave the censor the words for "When Irish Eyes are Smiling" but the censor threw it out remarking that the eyes did not smile, the mouth did! If we put mouth in he would allow it, truly believing that there was some hidden meaning or joke against themselves.

Henry O'Kane

Celebrating with bread and jam

Christmas (1940), my first as a POW, came and went. We got an extra ration of bread and jam to celebrate with. All the talk was of home and what our loved ones would be doing.

Frank Tayler

Like University with a touch of Broadmoor

Captain Alastair Bannerman sent a letter to his wife on Christmas Day 1944 describing celebrations in Oflag 79 near Brunswick.

Xmas morning and the sun is shining and the frost lies in patterns across the window. God bless you, my family, my heart is with you.

I went to a carol service at 4.30 yesterday and thought of you and Andrew and Richard having a tree and presents and I was very close. *O come let us adore him* I sang as if we were round your piano. In the evening we had a band show till 11.30 and then I went to Midnight Communion in the cellar that is our chapel.

What a strange life it all is here. Barbed wire and machine guns keep us in, but we make quite a lot of our confined life. A bit like university with a touch of Broadmoor!

This morning I opened my stocking (a sock!) with chocolate and snaps from you, which amazingly arrived on the eve. So lovely to glimpse you again, and so Xmassy to look at them by the light of dawn.

I've saved enough food to be really full today, anyhow, with fried bread and potatoes, marmalade and coffee for breakfast. (Red X parcels still trickle through, but I guess not much longer.)

I've been asked to read the lesson at 11.00 Matins, great honour! For lunch, pea soup and choc. Tea, I've made a cake (and/or pudding) from biscuits and prunes, and iced it with milk powder. Also painted a card symbolising our love, joining prison and Sandford Cottage across the seas and distance, pinned up over my top bunk. German stew for supper - ugh!

We're doing a *Round the Empire* Xmas show tonight in our underground cabaret *Xmas Pie* and I am appearing in a beard as the old spirit of 1944 saying good-bye to this year!

Some prisoners are spending their 5th Xmas "in the bag", a bit grim and hardly merry. But the news is good and they are very courageous and patient. It is very cold, no hot water, but have enough clothes. But do send pyjamas, towel, choc and toothbrush and paste if you can!

Your love and image is always my strength, and I thank God for many mercies. I love you.

Alastair Bannerman

Chapter 13

Death March

These were his servants, in his steps they trod,
Following through death the martyr'd Son of God.
Sir John Arkwright - O Valiant Hearts

I shall never forget

Fred Frost was 20 and serving with the Royal Artillery, when he was captured at Tobruk on June 20, 1942. At first he was reported as "Missing in Action" but, some three months later, his family were informed he was a Prisoner of War.

He was moved from one prison camp to another throughout Italy and ended up, in September 1943, being forced to work in a Polish coal mine near Gliwice, a town of some 200,000 in the Silesian coalfield, now part of Germany. He was, in effect, part of Nazi Germany's slave labour force.

As the Soviet forces advanced in January 1945, he was rounded up with other British POWs for a forced march of between 800 and 900 miles.

The Feldwebel *(sergeant)*, in a state of some agitation, came into the hut and told us that we were to be ready to move out at 9 o'clock that night. This really caused some excitement. Where we were going did not seem to matter, the all important thing was, we were leaving the mine, on what we could only hope was the first stage towards eventual freedom.

How to equip oneself for the march of unknown duration did not cause much of a problem. It was just a case of putting in all the clothing one possessed and carrying whatever food one had.

Thanks to the parcels received through the Red Cross I was able to don a couple of sets of underwear, two shirts, battledress and pullover, two pairs of socks, greatcoat and balaclava.

My only real decision came as to what boots I should wear. The heaviest ones were showing signs of wear whilst I recently received through the Red Cross a pair which I had hardly worn. The latter were of a much lighter construction, but would stay waterproof longer. I finally settled for them. Thankfully they were big enough to allow me to wear two pairs of socks.

Thus equipped, with two blankets in a roll round my shoulders and two old pairs of socks for gloves, I was ready for the road.

Of course all the other members of the hut were rigging themselves out in a similar fashion and, owing to the fact that all the fuel we had left had been used to stoke up the iron stove, we were sweating profusely by the time to leave arrived.

From the store the Germans issued each of us with a Red Cross food parcel. These had been packed in England as special Christmas parcels but, for some reason, had not come to us at the time. I managed to sling this over my shoulder using a piece of string I happened to have, and, at the shouts of "Raus" from the guards, joined the rest as we assembled in the compound.

The temperature was well below freezing and the frozen snow crackled under one's feet as we lined up under the floodlights from the guard towers to be counted. Two of our number from the sick bay were to be towed on sledges. I suppose that was the only form of transport available.

It was a clear moonlight night as we were escorted through the gates for the last time and went off in a westerly direction passing the slag heaps from the mine which were now covered in snow. They looked like a small mountain range.

We tried to find out from the guards how far we were going and what was to be our destination. The only vague sort of answer we got was that we had a five day march ahead. All the time we could hear rumblings and see dull flashes in the sky behind us and wondered if we would eventually be overtaken and, if so, what then?

In a little while we met German army units dressed from head to foot in white

---

OFFICE FORM NO.229B. (Revised).

Ref: H.A./NB/M/1802

Regimental Pay Office,
Gt.Central Street,
LEICESTER.

Dear Sir/Madam,

21/ 7 /1942 .

I have learned with regret that you have been informed that –

Army No. *1456524* Name *Frost, F. E.*

Rank *LBDR.* Unit *222 AA HHQ, REGT R.A.*

has been reported as missing.

You will doubtless wish to know without delay your position regarding the allowance/allotment payable to you until such time as further information about the soldier is forthcoming.

The allowance/allotment at present being paid to you on his behalf will be continued until *13.11.42.* at *18.6* per week, subject to any adjustment that may be necessary as a result of further information concerning the soldier being received before the latter date.

Should no news of the soldier be received by *13.11.42* , the rate at which the allowance/allotment may be continued will be subject to review and a further communication will be sent to you.

I am, Sir/Madam,

Your obedient Servant,

for Regimental Paymaster.
R.A. (H.A.A.).

To: *Mrs. M. Frost*
182 Bickenshaw Rd.
Abbey green.

Keeping the books straight. The impersonal note which Fred Frost's mother received about allowances after he was reported 'missing in action'.

snow camouflage material going in the opposite direction across the open fields to our left, while, along the road, came their horse-drawn wagons carrying their supplies. One couldn't help but feel some sort of pity for them going to meet the Russian advance.

After three hours on the road we were driven into a collection of farm buildings. Several of us went along a narrow path that had been made through the knee high snow and entered the darkness of a wooden shed. Here we found somewhere to lie down and try to have some sleep - not easy in the severe cold.

We were not given long before there were shouts of "Raus Schnell" from the guards and we were on our way again. As dawn was breaking we came to a line of refugee horse drawn wagons silhouetted against the sky as it drew lighter. There appeared to be no sign of life as the horses stood patiently. Maybe they had been travelling for some time and were exhausted.

We kept on the move all day, taking occasional rests, but sitting in the snow by the side of the road in the intense cold was no pleasure.

In one small village we were given hot water to fill our enamel mugs by nuns who ventured out from their home to see us. Later in the day we were halted at a lone farm where we had to find somewhere to sleep. There were five of us in our syndicate who, by operating as a team, had learned the art of survival in as comfortable manner as possible in the circumstances. After eating something from our Red Cross food parcels we settled down for the night, five in a row in the straw.

We found a sort of lean-to shed. We removed only our greatcoats which we spread out over the top of the straw and lay close together for warmth. Here I made the mistake of removing my boots and placing them together on the ground near where we were lying. In the morning when I picked them up they were frozen together with the snow that was on them. So Greg, one of our group, took them into the shed where the cows were lying tethered and somehow managed to thaw them sufficiently so that they could be worn by leaving them for a while in the bedding close to the recumbent animal.

Needless to say, I had learned an important lesson, not to remove my boots at night until there was a change in the temperature.

The second day on the march ended at another farm where the five of us quickly looked for a good place to stake a claim for sleeping that night. The top priority was always a cowshed where the animals stayed tethered. This was the warmest place. In any event plenty of straw was most important.

It was here that the German officer in charge decided that food would be required by everybody if we were to continue much longer. A bullock was roped and led out into the farmyard and promptly shot by one of the guards. In a very short time it was hung up in a doorway, skinned and butchered and, by that evening, there were several fires burning in the yard as various groups of us cooked, in a fashion, the portion of meat given to us.

It was at this farm that our group acquired an enamel cooking pot about 9 inches deep and 12 across with a small handle on opposite sides. Into this we put our chopped up meat along with a few potatoes we had found, covered them with water, and boiled the lot until it was all reasonably edible. That cooking pot became an essential part of our equipment for weeks to come. The five of us took it in turn to carry it, a day at a time, by attaching a piece of string to the handles and looping the string around the neck so that the pot hung in front of the chest.

A regular pattern was now emerging whereby we were on the road during the earlier part of each day and then being herded into some sort of farm or other buildings for the night. It remained bitterly cold with the ground covered in frozen snow for weeks on end.

It was not possible to rely on food rations from the Germans. Sometimes soup was cooked in boilers on the farms and sometimes there was an issue of bread. But we soon learned that we had to fend for ourselves as much as possible.

Each afternoon, when we had halted, the five of us soon had a fire going with the cooking pot heating the water ready to receive anything we could acquire from round the farm buildings, usually potatoes or swedes. Even boiled wheat was better than nothing.

Occasionally an unsuspecting hen ended up in the pot covered with a few potatoes to hide it from patrolling guards. It was a near thing one day for, as we entered a large barn piled up with loose straw, a hen flew up on to the top of the straw followed in quick time by two of us. The hen began squawking and making quite a din just as Greg grabbed hold of it. At that moment a guard burst in unslinging his rifle and shouting: "Was machen Sie?" Fortunately Greg had the presence of mind to hold the hen underneath him and sit on it in the straw thus silencing its protestations. As the guard approached we both sat there looking quite innocent without a sound. We celebrated that night with quite a meal.

It would be impossible to chronicle the events of the next three months in any sort of sequence.

The farm buildings in which we slept were much the same, distinguished only by the amount of straw or hay available to ensure a reasonable night's sleep, and, of course, the food which we were given or which we were able to acquire by some means or other.

Quite a lot of time was spent passing through Czechoslovakia where it was quite obvious that the local population was very much anti-German. There were occasions when some of the villagers would walk alongside our column and slip pieces of bread to us when they thought they were not being seen by the guards. On one occasion I saw a group of Russian prisoners who broke away to grab bread which had been left in a bowl on the footpath. Their guards immediately set about them with their rifle butts in an attempt to stop them.

Apart from the farms, we also spent the night in what was once a brewery and on the floor of a small factory, which appeared to produce wood wool for mattresses, and then inside brick kilns which took the form of brick-built tunnels with a layer of sand on which to lie.

February gave way to March when the cold became a a little less intense and the occasion arose when we were able to have some sort of wash.

We were housed in a ramshackle wooden barn by the side the road from which a grassy bank sloped down to a stream. In the spring sunshine we divested ourselves of some of the layers of clothing and bathed in the clear cold water. When I removed my boots and socks I was quite surprised to see that my feet were black and shiny, hardened by weeks of walking. Fortunately they were still quite comfortable in the pair of boots I had chosen to wear when we left the mine.

By now lice had become something of a problem and this was a good chance to deal with the matter. Our ablutions were interrupted when the guards ordered us back into the barn, the reason for which soon became obvious. Through a gap in the wooden wall I could see a column of concentration camp prisoners in their striped clothing being driven along the road.

It was a pitiful sight, particularly when one of them fell to the ground unable to continue and was promptly dispatched by a bullet from the rifle of one of the guards. Shortly afterwards two US Airforce fighter planes came in low over the barn and shot up a railway engine standing on the track about 200 yards away.

It must have, by now, become obvious to the Germans that our route to the west would eventually bring us into the path of the British and American advance, so we were taken on a southerly course. I have no recollection of place names, mainly because our journey was through the countryside, avoiding towns or large villages.

However, we eventually came to a village railway station where we were housed for several days. It was near the town of Weiden, about 50 miles east of Nüremburg. As we approached the town three or four American fighter planes circled our small column and then came diving down on us in line astern. We did not wait to ascertain their intentions but dived into the ditch at the side of the road. They roared over our heads and disappeared as quickly as they had come.

It was agreed that if they returned and carried out a similar manoeuvre we would stand our ground and wave in an effort to identify ourselves. Sure enough, they did come back, but as they came in at tree-top height we stayed on the road and waved frantically. This must have done the trick because they banked and came in again, this time two of them doing a victory roll over our heads. It was quite a relief to know that we had been recognised.

At the railway station a room between two platforms had been fitted out with two wooden shelves, one above the other, about 30 feet long, six feet wide and fastened along one wall. There was just room to pass along between these shelves and the wall opposite. It was on those shelves that we were to sleep for the next few days.

We were put to work clearing a path between the railtrack and the trees in the forest through which trains would run. Presumably this was a path to stop any spread of fire between the train's engine and the trees. The whole operation was a farce, we didn't really do a thing. The guards couldn't have cared less anyway.

We moved on again and, as we got into the month of April, it was, of course, much warmer although there was no improvement in the food situation. We were told there would be no bread because the bakery had been bombed.

There was quite a lot more Allied air activity by now and we met columns of German horse-drawn vehicles going in the opposite direction. So we knew that they must be in retreat from the British and American advance from the west.

Then came the great day.

There are few actual dates I remember from those days. But May 1, 1945 remains clear in my mind.

It was round mid-day when we had halted on a country road. There were open fields and some wooded areas around and it was in the field next to where I stood that I noticed the remains of a potato clamp. On investigation, I found about half a dozen small potatoes from which I wiped most of the mud and then stuffed them inside my battledress jacket hoping that we should be able to cook them somewhere in the evening when we stopped for the night.

As we waited, not knowing what was happening up ahead round the bend in the road, it began to snow very heavily with a driving wind.

Suddenly, round the bend came a number of our fellow POWs waving their arms and shouting for us to follow them.

The guards had disappeared. Apparently a bridge up ahead was about to be blown up and they had gone across abandoning us to our own devices. Needless to say the five of us set off together along one of the lanes, eventually catching up with a farmer leading a horse pulling a farm wagon.

Having just walked 800 or 900 miles, the chance of a lift was too good to miss!

The old chap did not protest. In fact he just continued leading the horse as we climbed into the back of the cart. On reaching the outskirts of the village we parted company and went to look for somewhere to stay that night. Eventually we approached a farm house and knocked on the door which was opened by the farmer who was obviously somewhat concerned to see these rather disreputable characters standing there.

We indicated in our best German that we wanted to stay there that night and told him not to worry as we meant no harm. Reluctantly, he let us in so we went into the large kitchen. It had a stone flagged floor, a table, chairs and a cooking range, but not much else. He left us but reappeared shortly afterwards with his family who gazed at us through a half-open door. We did our best to reassure them that they would be quite safe, at which stage they closed the door and went away.

The potatoes I had picked up earlier I washed at the sink, cut into slices, and placed on the top of the hot wood-burning stove. These we shared out for our supper before spreading our blankets on the stone floor and sleeping soundly in a real house for the first time in ages.

Early the next morning we prepared to move out, not knowing what the situation was, particularly as there were some bursts of machine gun fire not far away. Two of us went on a bit of a recce. By then it seemed quiet and along the road we met our first Americans coming into the village in a jeep.

Thus reassured, the five of us walked to the village to see what was going on. As we approached the one and only hotel I heard a hen cackling in the out-houses at the rear. I followed the sound and, sure enough, in a manger in the stable there was a newly-laid egg. I took it into the kitchen where there was quite a bit of activity as everyone seemed to want something to eat.

Fortunately I managed to get one of the cooks to fry my egg in a pan and then, with a slice of bread, I went into the dining room, sat down at one of the tables, and enjoyed something like an English breakfast.

Sitting at the far end of the room, around a table, was a group of uniformed German soldiers looking somewhat dejected. I felt quite superior in the knowledge that they no longer were giving the orders and that we were free to move around as we wished.

Later on that morning two of us met an American sergeant who asked us if we wanted anything to eat. We certainly did! We followed him through a farmyard and to the house and into the kitchen. We weren't the only ones with the same mission.

Round a scrubbed table sat a motley crew of individuals, some of whom I was able to identify by their uniforms. The British looked a rather rag-tag lot compared with the Germans in their smart field grey and jackboots. The Frau, a woman of ample proportions, placed a large bowl of soup with some sort of dumplings in the middle of the table and then it was every man for himself as we ladled it into our plates.

Nothing much was said until, as we were ready to get up and leave, it was noticed that the German officer sitting next to me still had his pistol in his belt. The British NCO on the other side of the table indicated to him that he wouldn't be needing that any more. The officer unbuttoned his holster and placed the gun on the table. It was picked up and taken into safe custody.

Fred Frost heard from the Americans that the war was over and, on May 10, 1945, started the journey home. He landed at an airfield near Brighton and, after completing formalities, made his way home to Nottingham

I reached the Midland Station and stepped out on to Arkwright Street in a bit of a daze. Was this really me walking to the centre of the town to get my bus? Did the past four years really happen? Three months at sea in a convoy; Egypt, the Western Desert, Italy, Germany, Poland, and an 800 to 900 miles walk through Czechoslovakia and Germany and then flights to England?

Suddenly I was walking along a street in Nottingham, passing all manner of people going about their daily business, as if nothing had ever happened. The feeling of freedom was strange. I was at last on my own, not recognising a single passer by.

I took the bus from Market Square on what was really the final lap. As I alighted at my stop a neighbour signalled to our house which brought Joan and my sister Barbara flying round the corner to meet me. Mother and Dad were waiting at the gate.

We were all together again in that wonderful moment.

Fred Frost

The homecoming

Stan Howes, who served with the 2/7th Battalion, the Royal Warwickshire Regiment, was wounded during the Dunkirk evacuation. He was captured and spent five years as a POW in Germany and Poland working on farms for a long period. On January 21, 1945, the German guards rounded up the prisoners and a column of 1,000 men were forced to march west in advance of the Russian attack.

The Germans did not issue any food at all which meant the lads were getting weaker and unable to carry on. I do not know what happened to them or the bodies of those who died.

So many humiliating incidents occurred on the march. As we went through villages people lined the streets jeering the "Englishe schwein hunde" and sent their children to spit at us.

The march went on towards the end of April '45, having covered some 800 miles in just over three months when the Americans liberated us. I think we were too weak and stunned to realise what had happened.

A batch of 20 of us were taken to an American field hospital where we were bathed and weighed. I was less than eight and a half stone after being thirteen and a half at the farm. After a fortnight of treatment we were flown back to England on a Dakota twin-engined aircraft, landing at Chisledon, near Swindon.

We were met by the Red Cross with a few cigs and chocolate and a free telegram to send home. Mine read "Arrived in England. Happy Birthday Dad". It was May 13, and his birthday, but we were not allowed to go home because of the state of our health.

A bus load of us were taken to Bromsgrove Hospital where, after good food and nursing, we were allowed to walk in the grounds and later down to the town.

This was a frightening experience. I kept expecting to be arrested and I went into Woolworths where I felt safe. At the sweet counter some Devon toffee took my fancy and I asked for a quarter of a pound. I offered the girl the money but she asked for the coupons which I hadn't got and didn't know about.

She asked if I was from the hospital and I replied, "yes," apologised and left. I hadn't gone far when she ran after me with the toffee. Free.

After two weeks I was sent home with six weeks leave. When I arrived home I did not recognise my younger sister who was a schoolgirl of 12 years when I left home in 1939 and was now a lovely girl of 18. When my leave was over I spent a further two weeks in Rugby St. Cross Hospital before returning to my Regiment.

Stan Howes

A will to survive

Eric Herwin was 23 and newly married when he was shot down on a bombing mission on August 12, 1942. He spent two years five months as a POW, mainly in the notorious Lamsdorf V111b Camp in Silesia where he kept a secret diary of day to day life behind the wire - with a radio hidden in a hollowed out Bible to keep in touch with the outside world. He was chained up for weeks on end and life was a constant struggle to find enough to eat.

Then he was one of a batch of 2,000 RAF men who were forced to march some 1,000 km (625 miles) from the advancing Russian forces. The ragged column of starving prisoners, brutalised by their guards, had to cover approximately 30 km. a day in the bitter winter of Eastern Europe. It is likely that many other columns were overtaken by the Russians.

Eric Herwin was one of only 23 RAF comrades who survived the seven weeks march to another camp in Germany. His diary, together with his reflections on the experience some 50 years later, makes one of the most gripping and moving narratives to emerge from the Second World War.

Jan 22, '45. Just ready for the mid-day meal (!) when we were given two hours to leave camp. Ours is the first compound to go. Heavy gunfire and bombing. Huns in a panic. Left camp at 2 pm with small kit only. Very cold and snowing.

We were in fact issued with a Red Cross parcel - one each - on leaving. I think they weighed 7 lbs. and we had to carry them by hand. We left in a group of about 2,000 together with guards most of whom seemed as apprehensive as ourselves. The senior guard (Captain or *Hauptmann*) had his bicycle. A horse and cart (like a covered wagon) preceded us. It carried off-duty or sick guards, their rations and kit, hay for the horse etc. The bicycle also quickly went on to the wagon as the Captain couldn't push it through the snow.

Shortly afterwards the Captain, who started at the front of the column, climbed into the wagon from which he directed operations!

At first the snow was knee high, but some days later it averaged 3 ft.

For half-starved men it was hard going and, even before we marched off, we were dropping like flies. Those of us who did get going were too exhausted really to carry their Red Cross parcels and some started to throw away the contents and also what was thought to be non-essential items of kit.

Stan Livingstone and I set off near the head of the column and I recall insisting that we hung on to the Red Cross food.

I left Lamsdorf with about 10 lbs. of stale chocolate. Chocolate had been sent me from home in clothing parcels over the years which I drew on occasions for escape and like emergencies. I have no doubt I was alone in bringing out such a large amount of chocolate for it was customary for 99 per cent of RAF prisoners to scoff chocolate as soon as it arrived from home.

In fact Iris sent me from home far more chocolate than any other RAF POW at Lamsdorf. Though malnourished I so disciplined myself on the rationing of what was available that I must have approached a stage of paranoia. Nevertheless, this near state of lunacy served me well in the last analysis.

I well remember later that day transferring half my chocolate to Stanley Livingstone with the strict instructions that it was to remain untouched till mine was consumed, the ration being 2 oz. each per day.

This transfer of chocolate was to even up the load as I was carrying the heaviest and, also, in the event of being separated, we would have some each.

Some 40 days later my share had been consumed (by the two of us) and when I asked for my 2 oz. ration he looked ill at ease and eventually confessed he had eaten it all. By that time our situation was precarious in the extreme. Our numbers had been reduced to half, many having died of starvation and exposure, dysentery, chest infections and other complaints.

Some were killed by the guards when they could not or would not travel any

Eric Herwin, the POW who kept a secret diary and survived a death march.

further. There was no provision for those too ill to carry on. As can be imagined, when I learned of Stan's conduct, my faith in human goodness fell to rock bottom.

Perhaps I should mention how I was clothed.

I took with me a spare pair of boots and some handkerchiefs. I left V111b wearing a size too large boots, three pairs of woollen socks, woollen underpants worn over long johns, two wool vests, two or three pullovers, wool gloves, oversize RAF tunic and trousers, a wool scarf to keep snow from going down my neck, a large nearly-new RAF greatcoat and a peaked cap made for me by Stanley Payne for just such an emergency. It was made from discarded RAF clothing.

It was cumbersome indeed, but, whereas many died of exposure, I only suffered from cold feet, hands, ears, nose and face. Even when lying in the snow at night I don't think I was excessively cold.

There was a will to survive.

Those who lost heart fell by the wayside and that included guards, some of whom were middle-aged.

I used my haversack as a pillow throughout, partly to prevent it being stolen, and I kept my clothing on for about two months. The greatcoat stank the most for it was well and truly smeared with diarrhoea one night when I entered and slept in a pitch black barn. We were indeed a motley crew.

Jan 23, '45. Marching continuously until 2 am. One chap died. No German food. Slept in a Dutch (open) barn. Some fellows frost bitten. Heavy gunfire behind us, estimated 25 kms. distant.

Jan 24, '45 Roads cluttered up with civilians fleeing west. Some terrible sights. Some of the guards have been hitting chaps with their rifles. Feet blistered and bleeding.

Jan 25, '45. Eleven men died in the snow last night. Fellows collapsing and falling by the roadside all the time. No one knows what happens to them.

Jan 26, '45. Still marching averaging 25 kms each 24 hours. Travelling W and NW. Bitterly cold. Snow and blizzards.

Jan 27, '45. Old Stan Livingstone is a marvel. One needs a good 'mucker' on this game. Many chaps killed by strafing Russian aircraft.

Jan 28, '45 Still going. At least some of us are.

Stan Livingstone was, to us, an oldish man. He was in his early thirties!

Jan 29, '45. Terribly cold. Only 20 km. today, but the going was tough.

A large party of Hungarian Jewesses on the road. Some lovely girls, but in pitiful condition. They were being flogged along by armed Hun guards.

These captive women (slaves) were being herded northwards and they passed through our column. Their guards and ours took the opportunity to bring us to a halt so that they could exchange news. We had in our party an American Jew who joined the Royal Canadian Air Force as a gunner - I forget his name but it will probably come back to me later. He was an eminent cartoonist and survived the war.

We halted for about 20 minutes in a place where nothing could be seen but endless miles of snow.

Some of the girls spoke to our Jew. The youngest was aged 13. They were the remnants of a much larger party most of whom had died on the trek from Hungary. They still had a long way to walk to their place of work.

None of the girls wore boots, their feet were bound with rags and sacking. They had been given no food for several days and our impression was that they would not last much longer.

The guards carried rifles on their shoulders and each had a stock whip in his hand. (Oh yes! I remember. Ernie Gershater was our American/Canadian Jew). Ernie was so moved at the plight of his fellow descendants that he could not contain his sobs and tears.

Events such as those are indelibly etched on my mind and they still surface in my sleeping and waking hours.

Jan 30. '45. The worst day yet. My right knee is in a bad way. Very hungry and have lost more weight. Can still hear bombing and gunfire in the west. We regard our officer guard and his crew as bastards. Many Russians and Serbians are moving in a similar manner to ourselves.

Most of our walking was along unclassified roads and across country. Overall our direction was West, but on consecutive days it could be S. West and N. West. At one point we crossed into Czechoslovakia.

All the evidence pointed to Hitler's intention to hold a large body of his enemy prisoners somewhere in Lower Bavaria as hostages so that he could bargain for a favourable settlement of the war but he was overtaken by the success of the Allied Forces.

Jan 31, '45. Resting today in a barn. No food or water. What a life. Stan sold his watch for a little bread.

In an attempt to quench our thirst we thawed snow in our mouths and swallowed. But we remained thirsty and our mouths and lips became blistered.

About this time our Red Cross food (the 7 lbs.) or that which hadn't been thrown away to ease the load soon after we left Lamsdorf, was exhausted. I remember the Red Cross tins of meat and vegetables so frozen solid that when we opened up the tins we still had difficulty eating the contents. I had a clasp knife and it was subjected to a lot of punishment.

Feb 1, '45. I reckon I may have lost over 30 lbs in weight. We all look gaunt and haggard.

Feb 2, '45 Made to march through small rivers. It has started to thaw.

Feb 3, '45. Over one third of the men who left Lamsdorf have dropped out from death, exhaustion or illness.

Conditions were such that a roll call was impossible - our column of broken and exhausted men must have been a kilometre long by day and night. The guards were also exhausted and trigger happy.

Feb 4, '45. Arrived at Stalag V111a yesterday afternoon. One ordeal follows another. This place is an absolute hell hole. Death from malnutrition an every-day occurrence - the Russian prisoners being continually beaten up. Almost 500 per barrack and very verminous. Met John Russell from Teschen, the camp badly run by the French.

While on the march I was unable to record daily current events. As a consequence, I cannot guarantee the date accuracy of the diary. The entry of February 4, '45 is a case in point.

V111a was a complex of prisons on the outskirts of Gorlitz (a town of 80,000 close to Dresden and the Polish frontier). On arrival we were herded into a Russian prison amongst Russians most of whom were without legs or arms.

We learned that the Russians were political prisoners and that this was an offshoot of another concentration camp.

The conditions were truly horrific. We were in a pen, about 50 x 50 yards. In the pen were three concrete huts, each of which should accommodate 100 to 120 prisoners. The huts were without heating and where there should have been windows and doors were gaping holes.

The huts were surrounded by a sea of mud. The hut floors were thick with mud. The layout was somewhat similar to a 1950s battery hen house. One slept on a rack or open shelf and the slats were entirely covered by a thick layer of the previous occupant's bloody faeces.

The bottom racks were, if possible, in an even worse condition because of the mud brought in on the feet of the occupants.

The pen was enclosed by barbed wire fences between which were the customary coils of barbed wire. The was no water laid on for drinking or washing.

We were left to rot in this place. No one with any authority would come to relieve our distress. We were so overcrowded that lying fully clothed on the racks one could not turn over at night.

The toilet consisted of a pit full of liquid faeces surrounded by a quagmire over which was an excrement-covered pole upon which one was supposed to sit. We were filled with despair.

Feb 5, '45. The strength of our barrack has risen to just under 1,000 - it is now impossible for everyone to lie lengthwise on the floor at night. The floor is covered in mud anyway. Managed to buy a little bread with my remaining few cigarettes. Never before have I dreamed that men could exist under such conditions as these.

A brief word about the Russian prisoners with whom we bartered.

Their concrete hut was next to ours but it had covers (sacking) over the doors and windows. All the Russians had at least one limb missing - either lost on the Eastern Front or since through lack of medical care.

The ones with one or no legs were without artificial limbs with the exception of one one-legged prisoner who had constructed a peg leg from a stick. These chaps seemed indestructible. They remained cheerful despite being constantly beaten about the head and shoulders by guards wielding staves.

Those Russians with two good legs and one arm were responsible for taking their dead outside the wire for a pit burial. The corpse was carried out in a rough coffin which was brought back for further use. It was in this coffin the Russians brought back the bread which had been traded for our cigarettes and other few precious personal possessions.

Feb 6, '45. There is one parade a day here - held in an adjoining muddy field in the rain at 7 am. What shocking lack of hygiene. The latrine is indescribable. None of us has the energy or initiative to do anything. Jack Woods and his brother have arrived and are in a bad state. Managed to get a 'wash' - very weak afterwards. Very little food today. My feet haven't been dry for weeks. If only my Cheale could see me now!

("Cheale" is a Cornish term of endearment.)

Feb 7, '45. Mud everywhere, the same old routine. Have developed a bad cough no doubt through being continuously wet.

Our numbers were increasing daily, not from the RAF, but Army POWs who left Lamsdorf after the RAF contingent. The guards kept on stacking the new arrivals into a building which was already overflowing.

With reference to latrines. On one occasion during the march I was the last one to use the latrine (a trench filled with urine and bloody faeces with a pole running its length for sitting on). When I had finished the young guard ordered me to fill in the pit with the spade and soil alongside.

I refused to obey and at that moment ignored the likely consequences. The guard unslung his rifle, put a round up the spout, and aimed at my head. He and I were about ten feet apart.

I cannot recall feeling fearful as I stood there making eye contact with the guard and, after what seemed a long time, he lowered the rifle and motioned me to rejoin the column, the end of which was still in sight.

It was not an act of courage but sheer bloody mindedness. Life was very cheap at the time.

Feb 8, '45. We sent a demand to the Internal Red Cross for a representative to be sent here immediately and also that, as we were not being fed and housed, we be sent to a neutral country. No doubt our letter will never be despatched. Meanwhile everyone becomes weaker.

I well remember helping to compose the letter to the Red Cross. It was in the form of an SOS. Whether we were successful in smuggling it out of camp is doubtful. With the benefit of hindsight I now appreciate that we were small fry and that our situation was the inevitable outcome of a near total breakdown of mainland European society.

Feb 9, '45. Rain by day and hard frost at night. Jack Woods has made us two handles for our 'mugs'. Theft here is rampant. Toc H in the evening. I am afraid I was bored. The Toc H spirit in this group is not very apparent.

It is interesting that though we were in a state of utmost distress there still remained a vestige of an ordered lifestyle!

Feb 10, '45. On the march again. Actually, although I feel feeble I am glad to be on the move. V111a is a terrible place under these conditions. We have been issued with one tin of meat (approx. 1 lb.) between 10 men and half a loaf of potato and rye bread per man. We are told it is to last for two days. I've a bad chest cold. Marching till 9 pm - a terrible night, 1,000 men in a barn. Sitting room only.

A word about the bread. At that stage of the war it was not unusual for it to be sent back in open trucks from the Russian front. Instead of being black it was green with mould, broken, wet and dirty. Rejected by the German fighting men, it was considered worthwhile transporting it all the way back to feed the likes of us. I imagine I can still taste the bitterness of the fungus and feel the wracking stomach pains that followed eating it.

Feb 11, '45. A fairly easy day. No further food. It's funny how one manages to carry on. Had my first row with Stan over the little chocolate we have left. I shared mine equally with him and now he won't give me any of his. A fair night's rest.

I can laugh about the chocolate now, but, at the time, it was a matter of life and death. I have long forgiven Stanley, but, as you have seen, I have not forgotten the incident.

Although I don't always practice what I preach I firmly believe that we should learn and be guided by past experience, hence I still tend to make provision for the future - whatever that may be.

Feb 12, '45. The Hun is supposed to be noted for his organisation. Ours is bad, but his is ten times worse. We appear to be going to Dresden. Finished the day's march at Bautzen and spent the night in the gymnasium of a very large barracks. We were given hot soup. The first hot food for over three weeks. If only we weren't starved and had dry clothing this march would be an interesting experience! Snowing on and off all day.

Feb 13, '45. The worst night's rest last night - terribly damp and cold - was coughing all the while, no sleep. Snowing this morning.

Feb 14, '45. We were kept waiting in the night for three hours for soup, and then told we'd had it. The waiting around for nothing, or almost nothing, is soul destroying.

Feb 15, '45. Don't seem to be able to shake off this 'flu. Am spitting a lot of blood and my nose bleeds frequently.

Feb 16, '45. We are getting a little soup about every other day now, likewise acorn coffee. Spent the night under canvas on bare soil - a group of Palestinians having pinched our straw.

Feb 17, '45. Crossed the Elbe at Meisson and then marched along the river's west bank. Stomach trouble and vomiting.

We crossed the river on ice which was rock solid. The rest days were for the benefit of our guards some of whom were middle-aged. Despite their regular meals and the fact that they were frequently reinforced they found the going tough.

Feb 19, '45. A fairly easy day's march. A food issue of a little black bread. Found that my little left toe has been frostbitten. The skin is peeling off in layers and it is without feeling.

Feb 20, '45. Was told today that our destination is near the Zeiss-Ikon works at Thorlingham.

The above information was either false or the destination later changed.

Feb 21, '45. We are now about 500 km from Lamsdorf and estimate the total distance walked to be 700 km.

Feb 22, '45. Finished the day at Dorma, a suburb of Leipzig. We were held up for over two hours before entering the town because of an air raid. Heavy anti-aircraft gunfire and many bomb craters. I appear to be recovering from the 'flu at long last. A dirty bastard has stolen Stan's and my bread ration (so tiny) for the next two days.

Considering our lifestyle self-discipline remained good at this juncture. Perhaps one in ten of the chaps had no thought but for themselves. Not bad considering the circumstances. Despite the cold weather most of the corpses we saw in the bombed areas were horribly bloated. They may, of course, have been dead before the winter set in.

Feb 23, '45. A long day. The 30 km. marches made longer by the complete absence of food. Had several partial blackouts. Passed through a badly bombed town. It was still burning and reminded me of my first walk through Plymouth after the blitz. A fairly good night's resting place. At least we had a light.

Feb 24, '45. Only 12 km today. Slept on the concrete floor of a partly built army barracks. Received one-third of a loaf of bread - my first for five days. I'm scared to look at myself now - am an absolute shadow. Saw plenty more bomb damage today. A horrible night. Had a long talk with F/Lt Jagers with a view to taking over command of the whole 4,000 Allied troops hereabout and fighting the Huns while we are still on our feet.

Jagers was just one of tens of thousands of prisoners moving around Europe at that time. He had become separated from his party and had latched on to ours. I doubt really if any of us had the 'press on' spirit necessary at that time.

Feb 25, '45. Marched and shuffled 36 km. today. Arrived at terribly overcrowded barn in pitch blackness. Blistered feet again and no sleep. Many fellows collapsing from exhaustion. Leonard Waterson badly beaten up by guards whilst in a state of collapse. He received severe injuries and has been admitted to a French POW Lazarette. (hospital)

Feb 26, '45. A supposed day of rest. No food apart from a little watery soup. Guards very nasty. I had a narrow escape from being shot. Feel very weak. We passed through Eisenburgh yesterday. The Huns appear not to know our destination. Chap shot for getting water. A lot more thieving. A cigarette case I was carrying for Stan has been taken.

A relatively small number of our "party" had only one thought - that of survival. Our circumstances encouraged this concept and, of course, we were no longer the 2,000 airmen who had left Lamsdorf weeks ago.

I would think we had, by this time, lost about 1,200 airmen and picked up two or three hundred men from the Army and Navy. We were no longer a cohesive body of men.

I should have mentioned earlier that our elected men of confidence, whose job was to look after our interests from Lamsdorf onwards, had deserted us early on. It is believed they found refuge in a hospital. The rot set in when they left their correct position, ie. marching at the head of the column, for a seat in the horse-drawn cart with the *hauptmann*.

In addition to German stores the cart contained about 100 Red Cross parcels. It quickly proved a temptation which our Australian leader and English interpreter could not resist and they immediately lost credibility.

They shared the Red Cross food with the senior German guards. This is not hearsay. I was witness to their despicable behaviour.

When the leader and the interpreter finally deserted it was left to a dozen or so of us (who were well known at Lamsdorf) to try to maintain a degree of morale within the group. Later on I was pressed into the position of leader, a position I didn't want as I was "knackered". However, I was given strength to do the job and an added bonus was a degree of respect from the senior guard.

Incidentally, the *hauptmann* who commenced the march with us, trying to push his bicycle, scarpered after two or three weeks, Had I been in his position I would have followed suit!

Feb 27, '45. A long day on no rations whatsoever. Many men collapsing, some of them beaten up with rifle butts as they lay unconscious. Got hold of an old cabbage stump and it tasted delicious. Had a wet dream last night - am terribly mad at myself but at least it shows I'm not impotent!

I well remember getting the cabbage stalk from a farmyard midden. I peeled the outer layer with my knife to remove the dung and chewed the pith from the remainder.

On another occasion (I may come to it later in the diary) whilst marching in column, I saw some forced labour women forking roots from a big clamp in mid-field, about 150 yards from the roadside. Without thinking, I broke ranks and half ran (!) to the clamp and seized a big swede . . . the biggest I could lay my hands on.

Meanwhile there was much shouting from the guards and a few rifle shots, one of which removed the heel of my boot.

Hiding the swede under my coat I regained the column where I was fearful the swede would be taken from me by a guard. But no such action was taken. At the first opportunity I cut the swede in half and gave Stan Livingstone his share.

Whilst going to and from the clamp I experienced no fear and no words of mine can express the lasting exhilaration and self-esteem I felt knowing that I had succeeded where others were unprepared to take a spur of the moment chance.

I wonder if I had the wet dream on the strength of the cabbage stalk. As a youngster it was not unusual for me to take a vegetable from my father's or some other person's field, rub the dirt off and eat it. I was often hungry and a between meals snack was most acceptable. It served me well as a POW.

Feb 28, '45. Left Jena very early. Terribly weak. The Huns have diddled us out of yesterday's bread ration. Climbed a very long hill out of the town - almost 8 km. long. A bit more shooting and the Huns again using rifle butts. Three chaps dying in the barn here this evening and the MO appears to be doing nothing for them. A little soup in the evening, just like hot water.

This must have been a stray medical officer we picked up - the first since we left Lamsdorf. We caught up with another who joined us at the end of the march at Ziegenhain. I saw this MO who opened his "surgery" sitting on a box in the open air. Told him that for a week or so I had been constantly dribbling urine. He said it was only to be expected and gave me an Aspirin which was the only medication at his disposal and he had but a few of these.

Feb 29, '45. A late start - 10 o'clock. Learned that the bread ration has been reduced by a further 100 grams. The civilian potato ration has been reduced to zero. My boots are almost finished. Learn that we are now en route for Kassel.

Mar 1, '45 No entry.

Mar 2, '45. Heavy blizzards. Lots of shooting and bashing with rifle butts, some more have died. A long day. Started marching at noon because of air raid and then continued for 30 km. over nasty country. Much bomb damage.

Last night heavy bomb dropped one mile from the barn and took off half the roof. John Brown has joined forces with us. Stole a little unthreshed corn. It tasted delicious.

Had it not been for the brutal guards our column must have borne a resemblance to that following the Pied Piper!

Our numbers were perhaps six to seven hundred at this stage - the numbers falling steadily because of death and exhaustion, but being maintained somewhat by odds and sods we picked up on the way. John Brown was one such. He was a big South Devon Royal Navy man. He was a good friend and as steady as a rock.

The unthreshed corn was wheat and had probably been saved as seed corn.

March 3, '45. Heavy snow. Marching delayed until mid-day because of an air raid. Three chaps shot. A real hell of a day - billeted in the dark. One-quarter loaf of bread, nothing else. Many men badly lashed with rifle butts for trying to get cold water - one guard in particular an absolute sadist. Saw much bomb damage.

March 4, '45. A day of rest in a badly damaged barn - no food or drink and terribly cold. Heavy snow. I was made representative of those in the barn. The vast majority of the 'occupied workers' we have met are as bad as the Huns. They take advantage of our hunger at every opportunity.

I was not elected as our group representative. I cannot remember the precise details but expect I was simply told by the men to "get on with it." There was a perquisite attached to the position of leader in that if there was enough for everybody, and by "enough" I mean about one-third of a pint of thin turnip, cabbage or sugar beet soup, or mangold, the leader was given a second helping.

This rule was enforced by the Germans to the end. It only referred to soup. At the end of the serving the soup would be cold, or almost cold, but an advantage was that it had more "body" than the earlier helpings.

Unfortunately we rarely had bread let alone soup and I can only remember getting my perk on one occasion. It was by the side of a high walled nunnery, built like a fortress. It had a leper hole in the wall. We held our tin to this as we shuffled slowly by and a ladle appeared through the hole into the tin. The soup on this occasion consisted mostly of pearl barley and, of all the meals I have had in my life (apart, I guess, from mother's milk) that small tin of soup was the most appreciated.

I have the number '65' in this diary entry. Sixty-five survivors! Incidentally, when I was ordered by the guards to collect my extra ration of soup at the nunnery I refused to comply, presumably because I felt I would be taking an unfair advantage. One guard in particular screamed at me and made to unsling his rifle and a weak roar from the men said "Take it." I complied and immediately gave more than half to Stan.

Don't ask me why! The occupied or slave workers were without any formal organisation or discipline. Their only thought in life was to survive another day.

Mar 5, '45. Very cold and much snow. Got lost over rough country and finished the day by doing over 30 km. 500 men crowded into a tiny barn inside which was a dung heap. Was standing up all night. No sleep. Several strafed vehicles about and here and there the remains of one of our aircraft. More shootings.

Mar 6, '45. Blizzards all day. Am terribly weak, my joints are very stiff and I get a lot of cramp, probably through lack of fats. Lips badly cracked and · sore. Haven't been able to change my clothes and only one wash since leaving Lamsdorf. One chap shot through forehead and others, chiefly the sick, badly beaten up with sticks and rifle butts. About 1,000 of our aircraft must have come over in the night. We are supposed to have new guards tomorrow.

Mar 7, '45. Issued with 125 grams of bread and 10 to 15 grams of lard, and we are marching 25 km. a day, sometimes more than 30. Another chap shot this morning. Our rations (when we get any) are now being issued in the evening with the result that we walk all day without food. A fellow (an Australian) was nearly murdered last night - caught in the act of stealing another man's bread. The Jews are a horrible crowd of animals, they live worse than pigs. Snowing.

The Jews serving with the Allied armies were a scruffy lot. They were mostly Pioneer Corps men. They appeared to have no thought for others; eg, some of the barns we occupied had substantial lofts floored with rough planking. They (the Jews) would urinate over the whole of the floorboards and their urine would be dripping on those below throughout the night.

March 8, '45. A day of rest. Half a litre of thin soup is the only food we've had for two days. Have had several more blackouts. Much bombing last night and today. Haven't slept for over a week owing to cramp and hunger. No medical facilities whatsoever. A chap in the barn died of starvation during the evening. Stanley Livingstone has confessed to not having any chocolate whatsoever. After him eating mine I feel rather bitter.

The latter part of the entry for the 8th hardly makes sense. But it's a wonder I kept any record! In extending trust one must accept the risk of failure. There were a great many occasions during the war when my life depended on the correct conduct of comrades. At the time the matter of the chocolate was life-threatening, and I expect Stan was too ashamed to admit to unethical behaviour.

Mar 9, '45. Received 230 grams of bread this morning, the first for three days. Many fellows can't stand. More blackouts. Marched 10 km., a great effort. Terrific bombing last night and again today. A lovely sight for tired and hungry eyes. A great many rockets sent up and very heavy flack. The Huns are putting out the most feeble excuses for our miserable plight. More shootings and beatings. Another bloke died. Sat in a heap of faeces whilst trying to find a place to lie down for the night. A good soup (considering) felt fairly full until I micturated five minutes later!

Faeces on hands and clothing, impossible to clean oneself, combined with all the other problems and I was in almost total despair.

March 10, '45. Heavy snow and rain. Crossed a range of hills. No food until the evening and then dished out of rations again by the Hun. Many beatings. Spent the night with the sick and felt reasonably good considering.

Food was available to us, but the guards would not let us have it knowing that in a weakened condition we were more easily controlled. It was on the march that I found I could get some relief from personal misery by trying to succour those unable to continue the struggle.

Mar 11, '45. Mangel soup from the Hun. Most chaps vomiting afterwards. Heavy falls of snow. Soles of my boots have completely gone and am walking on socks. Much trouble by Jews urinating on us at night from barn loft. Saw an aircraft go down in flames.

Mangel-wurzel is the plant *Beta Maritima* which is cultivated for feeding cattle. It was widely grown on farms when I was a lad. The roots were cut up like chip potatoes mixed with chaff and was the standard winter feed. Mangel, whether eaten raw or cooked, is rejected by the human stomach.

Mar 12, '45. Travelled several miles along the Autobahn. Noticeably little traffic. Very heavy gunfire from the West, a continuous rumble like thunder. Saw our camp site from a distance of two miles. On arrival first impressions were poor. Shocking lack of organisation. Put in charge of 65 men. So ends a march of about 1,000 kms. 186 men (part of the Sargen crowd) killed by strafing on the autobahn a few days ago.

At this stage of the war the autobahns were a favourite hunting ground for allied aircraft which strafed anything and everything, as I knew to my cost. On one occasion, marching through a forest, we crossed an autobahn which at that point was in a deep cutting. Speed was paramount in such a situation. We got down the steep bank and across the road all right, but some were too weak to climb the other side.

Ziegenhain was a transit camp, the accommodation being clapped-out non-weatherproof tents and marquees. The tents had straw on the bare ground and a water tap which sometimes functioned.

> **March 13, '45.** A cold and miserable day; rations here are insufficient to keep a man alive. A mixed camp - Serbs, French and Yanks. Busy getting things organised for my group of 65 men. This place is a real hell hole similar to Gorlitz. No sanitation, little water, no medical facilities. In tents on wet ground and very overcrowded. Heavy continuous gunfire and intermittent air raids. Have another bad cold but am pretty fit compared with others some of who are dying.

The camp must have contained representatives of every country fighting the Germans.

My group of 65 men were the survivors of the group which had made me their leader a week or so previously. I organised a list of the 65 by name rank and number so that it could be passed to the Red Cross if, and when, communications improved.

Most of the 65 were Army personnel, one or two Navy and the rest - 23 I believe - RAF. That is, 23 survivors from the 2,000 which left V111b on January 2. A copy of the list of names is amongst my POW papers.

Within the camp there were patches of ground where the snow had either blown elsewhere or melted and I searched these small areas for edible vegetable matter.

My effort was rewarded by a few dandelion roots one of which had a large gobbet of phlegm! I washed this and the other few roots under the tap and gave half to Stan. He was reluctant to eat them but I insisted he did so. I was also fortunate in finding a little green grass and rhizomes of couch grass which I chewed for their Vitamin 'C' content.

> **Mar 14, '45.** Weather is good for a change. Gunfire throughout the night. Tried unsuccessfully to get a 'bath' but managed to get a wash later. We are all lice infected. Had several blackouts. Air raids all day. Met a chap who lived at Fakenham and now lives at St. Budeaux (Plymouth). A small world. The Huns kept us standing outside for two hours in the evening. Our food ration today consisted of one-tenth of a small loaf of bread, half a pint of thin soup, half an ounce of margarine, and a half pint of mint tea.

> **March 15, '45.** We were issued with letter and post cards yesterday and have written to Iris and the Youngs. A very heavy air raid during the night. Still lots of artillery fire. Wrote a PC to Mother and one to Mum and Dad. Weather very good. Another man has died of dysentery and starvation, and

another RAF lad is dying in the tent. The dying are now being removed to a barrack where there is a doctor but little or no medication. Am still trying to organise representation to the so-called 'Protecting Power'.

Mar 16, '45. Rain throughout the night, much through the roof of the tent. The news service here very poor at present - little or no camp organisation. Artillery fire died down during the night. Yet another man in my group has died of exposure and starvation. A representative of the 'Protecting Power' had a look round today. Finding it very difficult to find men fit enough to carry rations due to weakness.

Mar 17, '45. Heavy air raids both by day and night. Am very doubtful if our representations to the 'Protecting Power' will bear fruit. The Huns will do nothing for us. Am making enquiries with a view to getting a job in the revier. Cannot sleep except for about an hour each night. Had a sweet given to me by one of the Sanitors. Am affected by a common complaint here - that of urinating throughout the night in my sleep.

Actually the Germans could do little or nothing for us at this stage of the war. They were on their knees. The thought of getting a job in the revier was little short of fantasy because the staff and inmates were hardly better off than ourselves.

Mar 18, '45. The Huns will not permit us to attend the camp's place of worship. Have acquired a decent radio and operate it within the tent. Two more men have died of starvation and exposure. Air raids and artillery fire last night and today. Have had to screen our 'shit house' because the civilians object to seeing our bare backsides!

Mar 19, '45. Delousing - took about four hours - very short of soap. We have some of the most horrible Huns imaginable here. They act as though they are dealing with the French, Serbs, and Ruskies (slave workers). Jack Hill and Fred Ames (two good RAMC chaps we picked up on the march) have now left us for duties in the revier. They gave me a few M&Bs, some sticky plaster, and a promise to keep an eye open re. a job in the hospital. Because some of our men have volunteered to work for the Hun the enemy is now *compelling* others to work for them.

The truth is that the Germans were more lenient with the French POWs because about ten per cent French POWs volunteered to serve in the German Armed Forces and a much larger number worked freely, without supervision, in German industry. The Serbs and Russians could also be persuaded to work for the enemy but should be excused on the grounds that they were not covered by the Geneva Convention.

Most of the POWs taken from Ziegenhain were taken out to open up bomb damaged roads and railways, and to construct defence positions; I can't imagine at this stage of the war that their puny efforts were of much help to the Germans.

Mar 20, '45. Flares dropped last night over the town by a medium size aircraft. Two bursts of cannon fire heard. A cold day. Huns very troublesome, screaming like spoilt children, knocking chaps about. Funerals today, five men buried. Hun arrangements for the burial awful. The number of dysentery cases seems to be increasing - no doubt due to lack of toilet facilities.

March 21, '45. Heavy frost last night. Very cold. First day of spring and the weather lovely this morning. Spent this morning shepherding my group. Heavy air raids last night. A number of Thunderbolts bombing and strafing nearby. They came very low over our camp and met with no opposition. Sometimes we are strafed. We have had 50 casualties in the last 24 hours - 14 killed. Many men collapsing through being kept out on parade for long periods. The war news continues good. Received a letter from Fred and Jack (hospital).

If I remember correctly Fred and Jack were RAMC chaps who were Toc H stalwarts at V111b.

Mar 22, '45. Another lovely morning. Raids and heavy gunfire in the night. Lockheed Lightnings bombed and strafed Ziegenhain in the afternoon. Nine aircraft involved. A nice fire left burning. Did a little sun bathing which left me very weak. A representative of the 'Protecting Power' came round and intimated that he was disgusted with the conditions under which we were existing. Two more men died of starvation and dysentery.

Mar 23, '45. A beautiful morning. Still sleeping badly - cold is awful, aching pains in my tummy. Another daylight raid by our single-seater fighters. News exceptionally good. Collected some dandelions for eating with bread. A lovely raid by Thunderbolts at Ziegenhain. Dive bombing and strafing. They appear to be after petrol supplies. A nice fire was left burning and there was little opposition. Parade lasted one and a half hours tonight - many chaps collapsing. Huns still trying to get POWs to work. A squadron of Hun fighters has arrived on nearby aerodrome.

Mar 24, '45. Weather continued good. Last night there was heavy traffic on nearby road and railways. Several raids by our aircraft on Ziegenhain and the nearby aerodrome. Montgomery has commenced his 'big push'. The most magnificent air raid ever in the late afternoon by Fortress aircraft on nearby aerodromes. An awe-inspiring sight. An excellent fire left burning. 300 Yank POWs rooted out at three in the morning to clear up bomb damage. Helped to dig a new latrine and had a blackout. We have no water these days.

Mar 25, '45. News is better than ever - our news service could not be better now. A lovely morning. Open air service. Lots of petty trouble from the Huns. A spot of sunbathing. Two bad blackouts. Air activity reduced to minimum. Trouble with tent Ration King. Must get him replaced.

During this period none of us wanted to do anything but sit or lie around to conserve our meagre energy - hence the excuse for sunbathing! However, I was well aware of the benefit of exposing parts of the body to judicious sunlight.

The Ration King for my 60 or so men was approved by me when, or shortly after, we arrived at Ziegenhain. I hoped he would prove a sheep but he turned out to be a goat depriving us of part of our food scraps.

Mar 26, '45. Rain on and off all day. Bombing and strafing last night. Bags of aircraft over today with fighters dropping their long-range petrol tanks over Ziegenhain. Bags of water coming into the tent.

Mar 27, '45. A squadron of Thunderbolts over today - no strafing nearby. Issued with a pair of clogs about three sizes too big. They are unwearable. Have started a group (tent) library with five books. Altogether a long hard day's work settling disputes and trying to fix up men (they include Palestinians and a Russian, French, Spanish and a Belgian) with the basic necessities of life. Poor old 'Lofty' Martin has just learned that he has TB, the result of malnutrition and exposure. The condition of us all grows steadily worse.

Mar 28, '45. Won a pair of long underpants - a second-hand gift from an Oflag. Weather cold and damp. But trying to care for my group - we are such a mixed lot there is little or no regard for anyone but self. Learned later that we are leaving here tomorrow to be marched to Mühlhausen which is some 110 km. distant. Received one-tenth of a French Red Cross parcel of food, also two American cigarettes, a quarter oz. of Yugoslavian tobacco, half a packet of cigarette papers and a box of matches! Didn't finish with affairs in the group until about 10.30 pm. The result of the small amount of Red Cross food was a nocturnal emission!

The march to Mühlhausen concentration camp never took place. We would not have survived the journey anyway. No wonder I didn't finish work until 10.30 pm. Imagine counting cigarette papers with 60 or more pairs of eyes watching to ensure they got their fair share. It is incredible, but it really did happen.

Regarding the "wet dream", I didn't know in 1945 that in order to maintain the species living things frequently attempt to breed before they themselves die. Needless to say, in our situation, we regarded such an occurrence as an unwanted waste of energy!

Mar 29,'45. Bags of stuff coming back from the Western Front all afternoon, evening, and night - roaring gunfire and explosions nearer. RAF and Yank aircraft (fighters) hedge hopped over camp yesterday. Pilots waved!! Most exciting. Am now in command of some 200 men. Am about the weakest of them all! Heavy rain. Some of our chaps together with other nationals are on the road again - marching. Decided to take a risk and remain behind. Haven't worked so hard for ages. The Russians are stealing our stores and I have had to organise a Camp Police Force.

It is likely that the German forces in our area were pulling back in order to reinforce the Eastern Front.

I don't know the reason why the enemy was in the process of moving us from Ziegenhain except that we were bursting at the seams, to such an extent that they had lost control of us as individuals.

Having a job to do, I thought it best to stay put at Ziegenhain for as long as possible and it was a wise decision. The few survivors from RAF Lamsdorf remained with me, together with nearly 200 others - mostly British. Casualties amongst those who left camp were high - mostly from strafing by our own planes.

Our meagre stores were barely worth stealing but, apart from this, we were determined not to give in to mob rule, particularly that exercised by our brave Allies, the Russians.

Mar 30, '45. No sleep last night. I now have 250 men in my charge and am organising space to accommodate them. Not easy. French must have been living like kings whilst we have been starving. Never before have I seen so much rubbish. The highlight of today has been the sight of Allied tanks and vehicles around the camp!! Yanks came inside and were mobbed and the excitement made me unwell. Russians behaving badly and we have secured arms for our guards (camp Police). The German guards have left but not before we searched them.

Ziegenhain was originally a camp for French POWs and I learned that some prisoners had been there since the beginning of the war. They all left camp on March 29, 1945. It was into their empty barrack that I moved my men. The place was in an uproar but the Frenchmen had made it into a bright and comfortable home.

There was evidence of Red Cross food in abundance having been consumed in the previous 24 hours. The bedding on the bunks was in disarray but I was fascinated to see the colourful blankets, quilts and bedcovers. There was an abundance of mirrors, empty scent bottles, empty tins of talc powder, pictures of saucy females. It was like going into an Aladdin's cave and fantasy brothel.

They were living the good life while we, their neighbours, were dying daily from neglect. I remember selecting a bed (as a perk I had first choice). I climbed on to it with difficulty and lay down. It was like lying on a mattress of eiderdown! In their haste to depart the French had left a tremendous amount of rubbish about, rubbish which little more than an hour earlier we would have considered treasure. We cleared it out, burned the combustibles, and installed ourselves.

We were now residing in a sort of no man's land with the Americans on the ascendancy and Allied fighter and light bomber aircraft in complete control of the air and searching for targets. One plane, a Mustang, with American markings, particularly attracted my attention and that of half a dozen other chaps with me in the compound.

It flew low over us and to one side once or twice and then turned and, from a distance of about a mile, made for the camp again, nose down. Sensing something was amiss I yelled for us to dive into a collapsed trench alongside.

While I was falling I clearly saw the aircraft's wings cloud with smoke followed a split second later by a long burst of cannon fire and a swathe of eruptions close by. It was a near thing!

Incidentally, when our liberators smashed down the gates to the camp I should have been there to greet them and hand over my section of the camp. But I didn't think it demanded priority! I already had my hands full, was not very well, terribly weak, and therefore unable to find any enthusiasm for our impending release and (writing with hindsight) lacking in balance.

I was certainly difficult to live with for a few months on my return to the UK. If the events described in these diaries had happened 50 years later maybe I would have been plagued by a team of counsellors!

The Yanks ordered us not to leave the camp to try to eat food and water because of the numerous nests of fanatical Germans (Hitler's so called werewolves) known to be active locally. One or two men did make unfruitful excursions into Ziegenhain.

Mar 31, '45. How strange it is writing in ink. No doubt I'll have to get used to it pretty soon. Rushed off my feet all day. Bags of Hun prisoners coming in. They were being treated beautifully roughly by the Yanks! They continually shout "Rause ya bastards, rause." There is no pampering, they are having to sleep in the open. It is good to see them draw their rations - looking just as I must have done ie, bloody awful. Too excited and billions of fleas. Our food ration has been slightly increased - bags of stomach trouble.

Despite what I wrote on March 31, very, very few of us sought revenge on those Germans of whom we had no knowledge of improper behaviour. I think all of us were more or less overcome with relief that we no longer had to struggle to survive.

Eric Herwin

After being liberated by the 6th Armoured Division of Patten's 3rd American Army, Eric Herwin was engaged in a great deal of form filling and getting new kit. Finally, on April 10, 1945, he flew back to the UK, landing at Leighton Buzzard and then by special train to RAF Cosford for a check up in hospital.

'Moments beyond description.'

Eric was one of 23 out of the original 2,000 who was liberated by the advancing Americans on March 30, 1945, my birthday, although I didn't know for a further ten days when I received a telegram to say he was back in this country and in hospital.

Those moments are quite beyond description.

He phoned me later that day - just to hear his voice again! I think he kept repeating "darling" and couldn't say anything else. On his return to this country he weighed 6 stone 4 lbs (88 lbs.) about four stone below his normal weight.

He was finally demobbed on November 1, 1945, on our fourth wedding

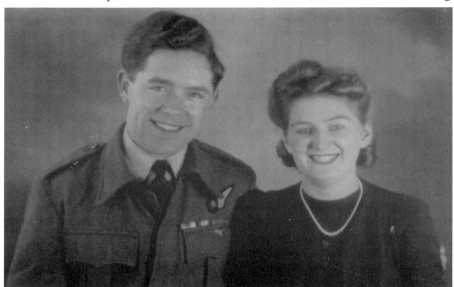

Reunited - a very special relationship. Eric Herwin and Iris before he was demobbed. He still wore the exclusive eagle Pathfinder badge on his tunic.

anniversary. Eric died very suddenly on our 57th wedding anniversary. We were blessed with something very special; we still remain as one.

After Eric's death I found in his wallet the following:

"Whilst a POW my frost bitten heart was warmed in the glow of Iris's love. It may be that I survived and helped others to survive because of that love. Without it, I couldn't have outlived the hunger, torture, and sadism of those years when the comforting embrace of death was irresistible to thousands of POWs.

"My wartime experiences must have affected my sense of values - like the effect of the sea on a piece of driftwood stripping away what is soft, leaving only the hard lines of the grain. It may account for my intolerance of self-seekers and opportunists and an impatience with their scale of values.

Supported by a personal background of exceptional quality - complete trust in my marriage - my morale largely depended on this."

Iris Herwin

Last Word

Ready and strong, marching along, Like the boys of the Old Brigade.
FREDERICK EDWARD WEATHERLEY (1848-1929)

I handed in my uniform and kit, receiving in exchange a civilian suit, a raincoat, a trilby hat, shirt and underwear etc. As I left the demob centre it was seven years since I had joined the Territorial Army for a fortnight's camp. It was seven years wasted in a way, I suppose, and yet I had learned a lot and had unusual experiences which I shall never forget.

Fred Frost (Slave-labourer)

My family experienced the hardships and consequences of war as we returned to our bomb damaged home, and yet, we unknowingly acquired the will to succeed and overcome.

Malcolm Allan (Evacuee)

I had a good war and was sorry when, in 1946, my father said I had to return home. I hated working in an office.

Vicky Hollins (Land Army Girl)

I hope we shall never see these times again. We must guard against it . . . the loss of life, limbs, and homes was quite appalling in this Midlands area.

John Carmichael (Blitz Policeman)

The column had halted for the night. A very ill soldier reported sick with a high fever and delirium. During the night he died and, at first light, was committed to a shallow grave. The column moved off leaving him alone, far from home, and maybe, later, a sorrowing mother and perhaps a wife. We shall remember them.

Dr. Ronald Bower (Medical Officer, Burma)

I was part of a close-knit team. How did you announce to your companions that you were frightened and would have to give up? The thought of having to admit to my father would have deterred me. No such intent occurred to me.

John Hadlon (air gunner)

166

Every day is a bonus. Enjoy it to the full.

Norman Schofield (Royal Navy)

I was incredibly lucky for we have evidence that the SS were finishing off wounded on the battlefield. I was captured by proper Germans.

Denis Dodd (Dunkirk survivor)

No one could have better mates and, in all, the bad times and the good, there were never any rows and we all looked after each other. Even when all ten of us had to live in one small room there was never any trouble. We always laughed at our trouble and enjoyed each other's company. At the end of the day each would tell about the things he had done and many a good tale was told.

Frank Tayler (POW)

As a fighting soldier in Korea in action I was scared most of the time, but it was war and one gets used to it. With comrades in arms I was aware that I had walked close to death. In the prison camps along the Yalu it was different. I was frightened, sometimes I was very frightened.

Henry O'Kane (Chinese brainwashing victim)

Looking back, I regard it as the best days of my life. I was fortunate, only suffering small spells in hospital but not through injuries.

Wilfred George Pincham (Royal West African Frontier Force)

We were all, Germans and English alike, in slit trenches and I found myself sharing one with a German lance-corporal. War seemed so unnecessary when ordinary men of each side could still be human and friendly. I hadn't met any Nazis then.

Alastair Bannerman (D-Day captive)

Our tour of active service was finally over and a lot of firm friendships were made. We headed back a little older and wiser and more self-confident in ourselves, each of us with a new outlook on life.

Ian Read (Borneo jungle fighter)

I return to the site of the massacre every year and relive those awful moments. I always remember the brave Captain who saved my life. As I walk over the ground I realise that he still lies there, buried somewhere on the site. They never found his body and the memories never leave me.

Bert Evans (Wormhout massacre survivor)

I think of it every day. The horror of May 29, 1940 and that barn is always in your mind. The years which followed it in various POW camps were terrible, but I have been incredibly lucky.

Alf Tombs (Wormhout massacre survivor)

Never before have I dreamed that men could exist under such conditions.

In my view it is impossible to convey to others the memories that still haunt us. Much better to push them to one side. One lived on one's inner resources with the deep assurance one was never alone, that loved ones cared and that God was there to sustain a purpose for living.

Eric Herwin (Death march survivor)

I know that those months on the march can never be fully described. Eric frequently had nightmares when he would be kicking and fighting in his sleep and bathed in perspiration. The answer, I knew, was to wake him gently, put my arms around him, and tell him that all was well. It never appeared to have any adverse effect during his waking hours. He was too strong a character to let it show consciously.

Iris Herwin (Wartime bride)

We had many mixed motives . . . no financial inducements, no share options. All started at a basic 2s 6d (12½p) a day. Although, looking at us now, you may not be able to imagine that we were all young once, there was a sense of adventure, a chance to escape from home, a chance to see the world. If we pooled all the travels of all the old men it would cover the world.

Rev. John Stanfield (SOE Officer in China)

Contributors

Eric Herwin Eric Herwin was Sergeant bomb aimer - second pilot with the newly formed 1st Pathfinder Squadron (35 Squadron) flying a Halifax Bomber when he was shot down and captured on the night of August 11-12, 1942. He was promoted to WO 1 while he was held in some of the most notorious POW camps and survived a 900 mile death march before being released in March 1945. In civilian life he went on to become National Horticultural Adviser to the Ministry of Agriculture, based at Wellesbourne, Warwicks.

Iris Herwin Iris Herwin met her husband two weeks before war broke out, when she accidentally knocked his pipe overboard during a steamer trip on the River Tamar. They became engaged in January 1941 and were married in November, just nine months before his plane was shot down. After her husband died in 1998 Mrs Herwin continued supporting village activities in Wellesbourne, including research into local history.

Norman Schofield In 1939 Norman Schofield was a butcher at his local Co-op. As a senior Scout he became a cyclist messenger for the ARP Controller for two nights each week. He taught Morse code, became "the enemy" for the Home Guard and in his spare time he raised and slaughtered livestock to help feed the hungry. In 1942, at the age of 18, he escaped from the killing fields of "civvy street" to the peace of the Royal Navy. They trained him to be an electrical mechanic to serve on what Churchill described as "that mighty ship Renown" - the only British Battle Cruiser to survive the 1939-45 War.

Fred Frost Fred Frost joined a Royal Artillery TA unit in Nottingham in the spring of 1939, when he was 18. He went off to TA camp in Norfolk with his unit 68 Regt. RA HAA and was almost at once deployed in Regular service as a L/Bdr. He served in North Africa, was captured at Tobruk on June 20, 1942 and was a prisoner of the Italians until Italy capitulated in September 1943. Instead of being freed he was taken by the Germans to camps in Silesia. From September 1943 to January 1945 he was a slave labourer in a coal mine.

Martyn Richards Martyn Richards, from Coventry, is a local author and playwright. He is chairman and producer for the Cofa's Fayre Players which aims to promote new works by local writers.

Ian Read Ian Read served with the Army Catering Corps from 1959 to 1971 in Malacca, Sarawak, Borneo and Singapore. He is actively engaged in welfare work with the Two Gates and Wilnecote Branch of the Royal British Legion and is the County Secretary.

Bert Hallett Mr Hallett, who was born in 1907, enlisted in 1926 and served with the 13/18 Queen Mary's Own Hussars. Subsequently he joined Warwickshire Constabulary and, for many years, was the village policeman at Napton where he is a life member of the local branch of the Royal British Legion.

Alfredo Ruiz Alfredo Ruiz came to Britain as a child evacuee from the Spanish Civil War in 1937. He worked in a munitions factory in Coventry during the worst of the blitz and when he was 18 joined the Royal Navy serving with Coastal Forces. He became a British citizen after the war.

Geoffrey Barwell, OBE JP Geoffrey Barwell served in the Royal Navy from 1944 to 1948. He is a member of the Corfu Channel Naval Association which commemorates the loss of 44 British sailors when Albania mined the Corfu Channel in May 1946. He was Warwickshire County President of the Royal British Legion from 1985 - 2000 and is National Vice President of the Legion.

Stanley Sheasby Stanley Sheasby a country-loving man, from Napton, Warwickshire, was one of four brothers who enlisted during the Second World War. He saw active service in North Africa with the Royal Artillery before being invalided out of the Army. At 91 years of age he still lives in South Warwickshire and maintains an active life.

Wilfred Pincham Wilfred George Pincham was seconded from the 7th Royal Irish Fusiliers in 1943 to become CQMS with the 1st Gambia Regiment, Royal West African Frontier Force. He returned to the UK in June 1946.

Alastair Bannerman Capt. Alastair Bannerman lived at Barford and, since his father was a former Battalion Commander of the Royal Warwickshire Regiment, he followed him into the Regiment during the Second World War. Mr Bannerman, a professional actor, was captured in the fierce fight for Lebisey Wood following the Normandy landings, was held as a POW, and subsequently went on to complete a successful stage career in the West End.

Bert Evans At first Bert Evans joined the Gloucestershire Regiment and, after 108 days, in September 1939, was transferred to the Royal Warwicks., the Regiment of his choice. After the horror of the massacre he was held as a POW in Poland for three and a half years before being repatriated through Sweden in October 1943. Because he had lost an arm he found it difficult to get a job but took up work as as cleaner scrubbing the steps of an insurance company in Birmingham. He became a filing clerk and eventually spent 32 years with Birmingham Baths Department.

Alfred Tombs After being taken prisoner, following the massacre, Alfred Tombs was held in German POW camps in Poland. He was taken to Lamsdorf to become a slave labourer in a coal mine. He was, however, suffering from a duodenal ulcer and went into hospital instead. When the camp was overrun in the Russian advance he was in Soviet hands in Austria before being freed. Mr Tombs was storeman at the Birmingham City Transport Department, Tyburn Road, for 32 years.

John William Slade John Slade joined the RAF in 1943 and served in Gibraltar, North Africa and India before being demobbed in 1946.

Stan Humphries Stan Humphries completed his National Service with the 1st Battalion, the Royal Warwickshire Regiment from 1951-53, serving with the anti-tank platoon while the Battalion was stationed at Graz, Austria.

Ernest Garwood Ernest Garwood served with the Royal Signals from 1939-45 in North Africa and Italy. After the war he returned to his profession as an ironmonger and then spent some time in Kuwait. He became a tool specialist with a West Midlands manufacturer and in his spare time took up youth work. Eventually he became a full-time youth leader.

Ronald Sheasby Ronald Sheasby served from 1944 to 1947 with the 5th Bn. the Queen's Own Cameron Highlanders.

John Whiteley DFC John Whiteley enlisted in the TA in March 1939 and volunteered for aircrew duties in November 1940. He transferred to the RAF for pilot training in July 1941 and became a sergeant pilot in May 1942. He taught the Army Glider Pilots to fly powered aircraft before they continued their training on gliders. He was commissioned in May 1943 and in December volunteered for Bomber Command. He joined 619 Squadron in October 1944 flying Lancaster bombers in a tour of 30 operations which included three 1,000 bomber raids. In September 1945 he was appointed captain of Dakota aircraft of 187 Squadron and was engaged on flying troops to and from India and Europe. He was awarded the DFC in December 1945. After being demobilised he joined the RAFVR in July 1947 and, in July 1951, was recalled to the RAF for 18 months as a flying instructor. He is secretary of 619 Squadron Association.

Ron Morley Ron Morley served in the Royal Navy during WW2 as a telegraphist. He was an active member of Knowle RBL for many years, serving as Branch vice-chairman from 1984-91 and as chairman 1996-97.

John Carmichael John Carmichael joined Birmingham City Police in March 1938 and worked in Birmingham and Coventry during the height of the blitz. He joined the Duke of Cornwall's Light Infantry in August 1942 and was commissioned into the 5th Battalion the Manchester Regiment. He was demobbed as a Captain and rejoined the police in Birmingham and retired in the rank of Superintendent.

John Hadlon DFM John Hadlon was a grocer's assistant in the Co-op and became a Sergeant air gunner serving subsequently with Pathfinder 637 Squadron, flying in Lancaster bombers on missions to Stuttgart, Essen and Berlin. He was awarded his DFM on June 15, 1943. Later he served with Birmingham City Police and retired in the rank of Superintendent.

Bernard W. Rushall Flying Officer Rushall joined the RAF in 1941, having volunteered for flying duties. He served as a navigator with Bomber Command flying Lancasters from bases in Lincolnshire. He completed 33 operations over Germany and parts of occupied Europe between 1943-44. He then continued as a navigator with RAF Transport Command flying all over the world. He joined the Metropolitan Police in July 1946 and left after 30 years service in the rank of Detective Chief Superintendent.

Mrs Elsie Rushall LACW Waknell joined the WAAF in 1941 and served in various parts of Britain until 1946. She met Bernard Rushall at a wartime dance at their local village hall. They married and have two sons.

Frank Tayler Frank Tayler served with the Royal Army Service Corps (now the Adjutant General's Corps) as part of the ill-fated 51st Highland Division which was captured at St. Valery, France, in June 1940 following the Dunkirk evacuation. He was held in seven different POW camps in Poland and Germany before being set to work as a farm labourer.

Malcolm Allen Malcolm Allen was four when war broke out. Barrow in Furness was an important shipbuilding town, producing surface warships and, probably more important, a considerable number of submarines. It attracted the attention of the Luftwaffe which inflicted considerable damage and carnage. Although he was not old enough to appreciate the full horror borne by his parents, he still remembers air raids, fire watchers, security slogans and the haunting smell of the air raid shelter in the newness of its bricks and mortar which became his bedroom.

Denis Dodd Major Denis Dodd was serving with the Royal Warwickshire Regiment when he was wounded and captured in the Dunkirk evacuation in 1940. He was subsequently repatriated to the UK and later worked in the War Office dealing with POW matters.

Beryl Pratt Mrs Beryl Pratt was born and raised in Knowle in the thirties and still lives in the village. She took part in fund raising through dances, garden parties, fetes etc., for the building of the Knowle Royal British Legion Club. Her father and later her husband were both ex-service and Branch members and she is still a member of the Women's Section.

Aubrey Chalmers Aubrey Chalmers, a non-practising Barrister, served as a TA Officer with the Royal Regiment of Fusiliers and saw Regular service during the Gulf War. Lt. Colonel Chalmers worked for the *Daily Mail* for 32 years as a professional journalist and he is Warwickshire County President of the Royal British Legion.

Derek Joss Derek Joss served with the 3rd Battalion, the Queen's Regiment from 1975 to 1986. He served in Belize among other places.

Cyril Reynolds Cyril Reynolds joined the RAF as a volunteer at the age of 18. He served with 194 Squadron during the whole of the Burma campaign from the siege of Imphal onwards, supplying and dropping troops into Burma, including the Chindits. He was also involved in the evacuation of the Railway Camps.

Bob Curry Bob Curry took early retirement from British Gas West Midlands where he was the Office Systems Support Manager. Having served as Branch vice-chairman he is Knowle Branch PRO and, since 1993, he has produced the monthly Branch Newsletter in which "Memory Lane" features members' service stories and anecdotes. He is a frequent visitor to the Somme battlefield and is currently involved in a project to erect a memorial to the Royal Warwickshire Regiment there. He also collects weapons and equipment from WW 2, which is displayed in support of RBL events.

Rev J. E. Stanfield Major John Stanfield served in the Royal Signals and was attached to the fabled Special Operations Executive Force 136 in China. After the Japanese surrender SOE closed down in China and he was posted to Hong Kong as OC Hong Kong Signals. Following demob John Stanfield spent four years at Cambridge University and was ordained into the Methodist Ministry. He spent seven years in The Gambia, West Africa, and then with various churches in the UK before retiring to Alcester in 1986.

Dr. Ronald Bower Dr. Bower served as a Medical Officer with Column 16, 1st Bn., the Bedfords & Herts., part of the 3rd Indian Infantry Division, in Burma and became a GP after the war. He was, for many years, a very active and enthusiastic President of the Knowle & District Branch of the RBL.

Clive Pitt Clive Pitt, PO/X105751, joined the Royal Marines in 1941 and served with the 10th Battalion and then in North Africa. He returned to the UK to join 48 Royal Marine Commando, landed on D-Day and served in Normandy until September 1944 when his Brigade was withdrawn to train for the assault on Walcheren Island on November 1. After service in Holland and Germany he was demobilised in February 1946.

Jeff Hollins Jeff Hollins enlisted in the RAFVR in October 1942 and, six months later, came to serve in the RAF. He trained as a WOP/AG and was posted to Syerston, Notts., for service in Lancasters. He volunteered for Special Operators in mistake for Special Operations and was transferred to the DCLI for a six-weeks culture shock. He was posted to the Royal Signals on the Isle of Man for training as a Special Operator and spent six months learning Japanese Khana. He was then sent to Italy for the remainder of the war as part of SOE "Y" Service which was set up to analyse and decipher wireless traffic in low and medium grade codes and ciphers. The term "low grade" refers to the degree of security provided by the code or cipher and it does not imply that the traffic in it was either unimportant or easy to break or interpret. Until his discharge in January 1948 he passed the time keeping tabs on Russian and Yugoslav communications from Italy and Austria, when not off training for the formation of a British Ski Division.

Vicky Hollins Vicky Hollins was evacuated to South Wales immediately before war broke out in September 1939 and she stayed on and became a member of the Women's Land Army. She returned to her home in Birmingham in 1948.

John Curtis John Curtis joined the Royal Marines early in 1942 and, after completing a signals course, was posted to the Middle East to join *HMS Orion* in Alexandria, part of 5th Cruiser Squadron. He served with the *Orion* during the Salerno and Anzio landings in 1944 and later at Normandy. After the war he returned to the family bakery and became Standard Bearer for Knowle Branch of the Royal British Legion.

Henry O'Kane In 1947, when he was 17, Henry O'Kane joined the Inniskillen Fusiliers as a Regular soldier. He was posted to the 1st Battalion, Royal Ulster Rifles which was part of the 29th Independent Infantry Brigade in Korea. He was captured by the Chinese and spent two and a half years as a POW before being released in the autumn of 1953. Following his time in POW camps Mr O'Kane was medically discharged from the Army in 1954. He is secretary of the Hatton & District Branch of the Royal British Legion.

Roy Scott At the age of 18 Roy Scott was with a Royal Artillery regiment at TA camp in August 1939 when he was mobilised on September 1. He served with a heavy anti-aircraft unit near Plymouth and, in April 1941, volunteered for aircrew duties. He trained in England and Canada where he got his wings and was commissioned. After a spell as a staff pilot at a bombing and gunnery school, he and his crew joined 295 Squadron, 38 Group RAF, a special duties Squadron flying from RAF Harwell, Oxfordshire, and later from RAF Rivenhall, Essex. Squadron Leader Scott was President of the Baddesley Ensor Branch of the Royal British Legion from 1968 to 2001.

Margaret Sharrott. Corporal Margaret Sharrott joined the WAAF in 1942. She was trained as a Clerk Special Duties - a plotter at RAF No 9 Group HQ, Barton Hall, Preston. She plotted the movement of all aircraft, both the RAF and the enemy. Later she was transferred to Netheravon, on Salisbury Plain, where the glider pilots were trained, then to Marks Hall, HQ 38 Group RAF. Eventually, as a Corporal, she was at the flying control tower at Rivenhall, Essex, where she met Flt. Lt. Roy Scott when he was in charge of night flying. They were married in September 1946. For a number of years Mrs Scott has been President of the Ladies Section of Baddesley Ensor Royal British Legion.

Stan Howes. Stan Howes joined the Royal Warwickshire Regiment in 1939 and was wounded during the Dunkirk evacuation. He spent the rest of the war as a POW and survived an 800-mile death march which covered a period of three months.